Mary Engelbreit's
Dining Out
Cookbook

Mary Engelbreit's
Dining Out
Cookbook

Illustrated by Mary Engelbreit

Photographs by Mark Thomas

Andrews McMeel Publishing

Kansas City

www.andrewsmcmeel.com

www.maryengelbreit.com

 is a registered trademark of Mary Engelbreit Enterprises, Inc.

Library of Congress Cataloging-in-Publication Data

Englebreit, Mary.

Mary Engelbreit's dining out cookbook / illustrated by Mary Engelbreit ;
photographs by Mark Thomas.-- 1st U.S. ed.

p. cm.

Includes index.

ISBN 0-7407-1500-3 (hardcover)

1. Outdoor cookery. 2. Entertaining. I. Title: Dining out cookbook. II. Title.

TX823 .E534 2001

641.5'78--dc21   00-052770

First U.S. Edition

01 02 03 MON 10 9 8 7 6 5 4 3 2 1

Recipe developers: Judith Sutton & Lori Longbotham
Designer: Amy Henderson

Produced by Smallwood & Stewart, Inc., New York City

contents

introduction

Want to know my favorite shortcut to making a good meal great? Just take it outdoors. Even an ordinary peanut butter and jelly sandwich seems like something special if you enjoy it with a view of a lovely tree or babbling brook.

Far too often, people reserve dining alfresco for special occasions—and only in summer. This book encourages you to "dine out," even in the middle of the week. With the exception of winter (unless you live in a warm climate), most of the year is perfect for eating outdoors. Think autumn picnic with a Thermos of hearty soup and freshly baked bread tied up in a tea towel or a spring garden luncheon featuring baby vegetables. Create some new family traditions: for instance, a post-soccer-practice patio lunch or Saturday noontime flea-marketing brunch in the gazebo. When you spend more time outdoors, you create an away-on-vacation feeling in your life every day.

If you expect that dining outdoors means planning a buffet of twenty dishes, then check out some of our menus. You could take a few appetizers and drinks to the garden or just enjoy a simple lunch of sandwiches. But we don't neglect the big events. There are lots of suggestions for themed parties. Potting-shed buffet, anyone? July 4th dessert party? I guarantee they'll provide a springboard for your own creativity.

Happy dining out!

Mary

chapter one

appetizers

grilled
ginger-garlic bread

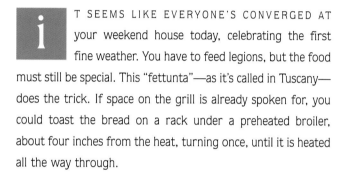

IT SEEMS LIKE EVERYONE'S CONVERGED AT your weekend house today, celebrating the first fine weather. You have to feed legions, but the food must still be special. This "fettunta"—as it's called in Tuscany—does the trick. If space on the grill is already spoken for, you could toast the bread on a rack under a preheated broiler, about four inches from the heat, turning once, until it is heated all the way through.

½ cup (1 stick) unsalted butter, at room temperature

3 garlic cloves, coarsely chopped

1 tablespoon finely minced peeled ginger

¼ teaspoon salt

Pinch of ground red pepper

1 loaf long, thin French or Italian bread

1. Preheat the grill to medium-high.

2. In a small bowl, stir together the butter, garlic, ginger, salt, and ground red pepper.

3. With a sharp knife, split the bread in half lengthwise. Spread the butter mixture onto the cut sides of the loaf and put the halves back together. Wrap tightly in foil.

4. Grill the bread, turning occasionally, for 10 to 15 minutes, until heated through. Unwrap, cut the bread into slices, and serve immediately.

Serves 8

■ Variations

For an infusion of nutty sesame flavor, add 1 tablespoon of toasted sesame seeds or 1 tablespoon of toasted sesame oil to the butter mixture. Or, for some zing, add 2 tablespoons of grated lemon zest. To the main recipe or either of these two variations, stir in 1 scallion, finely minced.

bruschetta
with tomato & olives

WHEN YOUR GARDEN IS POPPING WITH tomatoes, get on the phone and invite friends over for this delectable starter. We call it an appetizer, but we've seen people fill up on bruschetta to the exclusion of all else—it's the essence of summer. Double or triple the recipe, and you can really feed a crowd at a cocktail party or a buffet dinner. For color variation, toss in a few yellow tomatoes or some opal basil. For more pungency, add a minced shallot.

3 large ripe tomatoes, peeled, seeded,
   and finely diced
Salt, to taste
¼ cup extra-virgin olive oil
3 tablespoons chopped pitted Mediterranean black
   and/or green olives
3 tablespoons finely slivered fresh basil
2 tablespoons minced fresh parsley
2 garlic cloves, minced
Freshly ground pepper, to taste
Twelve ½-inch-thick slices French or Italian bread,
   grilled or broiled

1. In a colander, season the tomatoes with salt, stir, and let them drain for about 45 minutes.

2. Meanwhile, in a medium bowl, combine the oil, olives, basil, parsley, and garlic until well mixed. Season with salt and pepper. Add the tomatoes to the oil mixture, and stir to combine.

3. Evenly divide the tomato mixture among the bread slices and serve.

Serves 4 to 6

herbed goat cheese
on baguette toasts

yES, YOU COULD BUY YOUR GOAT CHEESE "preherbed," but freshly chopped herbs really give tangy goat cheese a delicious boost. You don't have to stick to this recipe: Instead, try an herbes de Provence mixture like lavender, thyme, rosemary, and summer savory. Though creamy Montrachet goat cheese is divine, you could also go with smooth and light Charvours from the south of France, or try the buttery flavor of Boucheron. To make the presentation as pretty as it is delicious, cut the log of goat cheese in two, roll one half-log in half the herbs and the other in half the spices in the variation (see below) and serve on a platter sprinkled with herbs; surround with the baguette toasts. Perfect with Zinfandel or Chardonnay!

HERBED GOAT CHEESE

I tablespoon finely chopped fresh chives

I tablespoon finely chopped fresh flat-leaf parsley

I tablespoon finely chopped fresh rosemary

One 11-ounce log Montrachet or other creamy
goat cheese

One long, thin French baguette, cut on the diagonal
into ⅜-inch-thick slices

About 3 tablespoons olive oil

1. Prepare the herbed goat cheese: Combine the herbs in a small bowl and mix well. Spread the herb mixture on a flat plate and gently roll the goat cheese in the herbs, coating evenly and patting lightly so they adhere. The goat cheese can be prepared in advance early in the day and stored, covered, in the refrigerator. Bring to room temperature before serving.

2. Preheat the grill to medium-high.

3. Lightly brush the slices of bread on both sides with oil. Grill, turning once, until lightly toasted, about 2 minutes on each side. Serve the warm toasts immediately with the goat cheese.

Serves 8

■ Spiced Goat Cheese

Reduce the amount of chives to 2 teaspoons and omit the parsley and rosemary. Sprinkle the chives, 1 teaspoon red pepper flakes, and 1 teaspoon coarsely ground pepper evenly over the plate, then roll the cheese in the mixture, pressing lightly so the spices and chives adhere. Serve with the warm toasts.

middle eastern
hummus & pita platter

eVERYTHING TASTES BETTER WHEN IT COMES off the grill—even pita bread. Team it up with this Middle Eastern–style dip and Warm Grilled Salad of Red Onion & Tomato (page 36) for a light lunch. Center the hummus on a colorful platter and arrange the pita wedges in a starburst. Tahini, a sesame-seed paste, is available in supermarkets; once you've opened the jar, keep it refrigerated.

4 garlic cloves, peeled

One 15- to 19-ounce can chickpeas,
    rinsed and drained

2 tablespoons tahini

1 teaspoon grated lemon zest

3 tablespoons fresh lemon juice

3 tablespoons olive oil

½ teaspoon salt, or to taste

⅛ teaspoon ground red pepper, or to taste

½ teaspoon paprika

2 tablespoons chopped fresh cilantro (optional)

8 pitas

1. In a small saucepan, bring 2 cups of water to a boil over high heat. Add the garlic and boil, uncovered, for 3 minutes. Drain the garlic and set aside to cool.

2. In the bowl of a food processor, puree the garlic, chickpeas, tahini, lemon zest, lemon juice, oil, salt, ground red pepper, and 2 tablespoons of water.

3. Transfer the mixture to a platter and sprinkle with paprika and cilantro, if desired.

4. Preheat the grill to medium-high. Grill the pita for 1 to 2 minutes, turning once, until lightly browned. Cut each pita into 8 wedges and serve immediately with the hummus.

Serves 8

Appetizer Accents

• Tuck fresh blossoms into water-filled florist's vials and nestle the tubes on a platter.

• Sprinkle with carrot "daisies": Peel and trim carrots, then use a mushroom fluter to cut furrows down the length of each carrot. Slice into little "daisies."

• Create a citrus ice "bowl" for serving chilled shrimp: Freeze ½ inch distilled water in a ring mold just until a thin layer of ice forms. Break the surface and slip in thin slices of lemon and lime. Fill the mold with distilled water and freeze until solid.

grill-sweetened bell peppers

SERVED WITH SLICES OF FRESH MOZZARELLA or topped with feta, basil, and chopped olives, this easy appetizer is destined to become one of your signature dishes. The next time you're grilling, make a few extra peppers and seal them in an airtight container—they'll keep, refrigerated, for several days. When it's six o'clock on a weeknight and dinner's running late, it's a lifesaver to be able to pull these treats out of the refrigerator to add to a salad, top a pizza, or toss with sausage and pasta.

> 1 each red, yellow, and orange bell pepper, cored, halved, and seeded
> 3 tablespoons olive oil, preferably extra-virgin
> 1 tablespoon finely chopped fresh parsley
> 1 tablespoon balsamic or red wine vinegar
> 1 garlic clove, minced
> ¼ teaspoon salt
> Pinch of freshly ground pepper

1. Preheat the grill to medium-high.

2. Place the bell peppers, inner side down, on the grill and cook, turning with tongs, for about 15 minutes, or until softened and with dark brown grill marks. Transfer the peppers to a cutting board and let them cool. When cool enough to handle, cut the peppers into ¾-inch-wide strips.

3. In a medium bowl, whisk together the oil, parsley, vinegar, garlic, salt, and pepper.

4. Add the peppers to the oil mixture, toss to coat well, and transfer to a serving plate. Let the peppers stand at room temperature until ready to serve.

Serves 4 to 6

■ Variations

Use whatever color peppers suits your fancy—a mix looks great, but so does a plate of peppers all in one color. Feel free to sprinkle the grilled peppers with crumbled feta cheese, pitted green or black Mediterranean olives, capers, finely shredded fresh basil or sage, and/or anchovies in any combination you choose. Remember, there are no mistakes to make here—just use amounts that look appetizing to you.

rendezvous in the garden
cocktails alfresco

even if you're serving the main course indoors, tweak the dinner party routine by having drinks and appetizers out-of-doors. The key is to choose an interesting spot in the garden—perhaps a grove you've strung with paper lanterns or a section planted with white flowers that glow all the more as the sun dips.

PERFECT FOR A PLATTER

bruschetta with tomato & olives
(page 11)

herbed goat cheese on baguette toasts
(page 12)

blue-cheese endive boats
(page 21)

silver-dollar crab cakes
(page 24)

GRILLED FINGER FOOD

grilled ginger-garlic bread
(page 10)

parmesan polenta squares with caprese salad
(page 18)

grilled jerk chicken wings
(page 23)

spicy sirloin satay
(page 23)

adobo shrimp pick-up sticks
(page 26)

NO-COOK APPETIZERS

full-length carrot sticks and store-bought breadsticks offered in glass tumblers or celery vases

three bowls of different olives garnished with rosemary sprigs

a platter of cheeses sprinkled with pecans and dried cherries, with a sliced baguette instead of crackers

Match the Mood

Set up an inventive buffet that coordinates with the look of your yard.

- In an area planted with ornamental grasses, rattan trays and wicker-wrapped bottles suit the "natural" theme. Bamboo tiki torches would work well, too.

- For a flower-filled border or rose garden, bring out your petal-theme china and knick-knacks. Use a retro rose-printed tablecloth and prop a trellis or two behind the buffet.

- Make a woodland bower seem enchanted: Hang charms, like stars and flea-market-find chandelier crystals, from tree branches.

parmesan polenta squares
with caprese salad

tRY THIS ONE FOR YOUR KID'S HIGH SCHOOL graduation, where at least half the guests will profess vegetarianism. Polenta isn't just the soft and creamy stuff you've come to know. We chill it, cut it in triangles, and grill it. The secret to making it especially delicious is Parmesan cheese.

PARMESAN POLENTA

1¼ teaspoons salt

1½ cups yellow cornmeal

4 tablespoons (½ stick) unsalted butter, cut into 4 pieces, at room temperature

¼ cup freshly grated Parmesan cheese

CAPRESE SALAD

3 large tomatoes, cut into ¼-inch dice

2 garlic cloves, minced

1 tablespoon olive oil

¼ pound fresh mozzarella, preferably salted, cut into ¼-inch dice

3 tablespoons finely chopped fresh basil or chives

Salt and freshly ground pepper

Olive oil, for brushing

1. Make the Parmesan polenta: Generously butter a 13- x 9-inch baking pan. In a large heavy saucepan, bring 4 cups of water to a boil over medium heat. Reduce the heat to medium-low and add the salt. Drizzle in the cornmeal in a slow, steady stream, whisking constantly to prevent lumps from forming. Cook, stirring frequently with the wooden spoon, until the polenta is very thick and pulls away from the sides of the pan, 15 to 20 minutes. Remove from the heat.

2. Immediately add the butter to the polenta, stirring vigorously with a wooden spoon until the butter is melted and the polenta is smooth. Stir in the Parmesan. Pour the polenta into the prepared baking pan, spreading it evenly and smoothing the top with a rubber spatula. Let cool slightly, then cover with plastic wrap and refrigerate for 1 to 2 hours, until cold and firm. The polenta can be made up to 2 days ahead.

3. Make the caprese salad: In a medium bowl, combine the tomatoes, garlic, and oil, stirring gently to combine. Add the mozzarella and basil, stirring gently to combine. Season to taste with salt and pepper. Set aside at room temperature for 30 minutes to allow the flavors to blend.

4. Preheat the grill to medium-high.

5. Cut the polenta into 8 squares, then cut each square diagonally in half to make 2 triangles. Remove the polenta triangles from the baking pan and brush on both sides with oil.

6. Grill the polenta, turning once, for 5 to 7 minutes, until heated through. Arrange 2 triangles on each plate, spoon some of the tomatoes over the top, and serve immediately.

Serves 8

picnic-style
deviled eggs

aPPETIZERS MAY COME AND GO, BUT DEVILED eggs are forever. Packed in refrigerator glass, they add a retro note to a table spread with a fifties "Souvenir of Florida" tablecloth.

12 large eggs

2 to 3 tablespoons apple cider vinegar

¼ cup mayonnaise

¼ cup sour cream

2 teaspoons Dijon mustard

½ teaspoon salt

¼ teaspoon freshly ground pepper

3 tablespoons finely chopped fresh parsley plus
**   additional sprigs, for garnish**

1. In a Dutch oven, bring the eggs, 1 tablespoon vinegar, and enough cool water to cover the eggs to a full boil over high heat. Boil the eggs for 10 minutes. Place the Dutch oven under cold running water until the eggs are cool.

2. Peel the eggs and slice them in half lengthwise. Carefully remove the yolks with a teaspoon and transfer them to the bowl of a food processor. Add 1 tablespoon of the vinegar, the mayonnaise, sour cream, mustard, salt, and pepper and process until smooth. (Alternatively, in a bowl, mash the ingredients together with a fork.) Add some or all of the remaining vinegar, by the teaspoon, to taste. Transfer the mixture to a bowl and stir in the chopped parsley.

3. Fill each half egg white with 1 heaping teaspoon of the filling, mounding it in the center. Chill the deviled eggs.

4. To serve, arrange the deviled eggs on a bed of parsley sprigs and serve immediately.

Serves 8

blue-cheese
endive boats

tHE KIDS ARE AWAY AT CAMP AND FRIENDS are coming for drinks and dinner. Tonight, the cheese doesn't have to be orange and square. Seize the moment to indulge in a French blue, such as a mild Roquefort. The pleasantly bitter edge of endive makes a perfect complement to the smoothness of the cheese. You can substitute heavy cream or half-and-half for the milk, if you like. For an alternative garnish, sprinkle the "boats" with chopped pecans or walnuts. This hors d'oeuvre is wonderful paired on a platter with Silver-Dollar Crab Cakes (page 24).

4 large heads Belgian endive

BLUE-CHEESE FILLING
6 ounces blue cheese, at room temperature
5 to 6 tablespoons milk
Freshly ground pepper

Minced fresh chives or chives with blossoms,
    for garnish

1. Trim off the bottom of each endive and discard any discolored outer leaves. Carefully remove 8 leaves from each endive (reserve the remaining leaves for another use). If necessary, trim the bottoms so the leaves are about 4 inches long. Wrap the leaves in a slightly damp paper towel and keep them in a plastic bag, refrigerated, until ready to use.

2. Make the blue-cheese filling: Crumble the cheese into the bowl of a food processor. Add 5 tablespoons milk and process until smooth and creamy, adding up to 1 additional tablespoon milk, if necessary. Season with pepper to taste and blend well.

3. Using a pastry bag fitted with a small star tip, pipe about 2 inches of the cheese mixture along the inside of each endive leaf; alternatively, use a teaspoon to mound about 1½ teaspoons of the cheese mixture onto the bottom end of each leaf. Sprinkle the minced chives or lay the chive blossoms over the cheese. Arrange the leaves on a platter and serve immediately.

Serves 8

■ Herbed-Cheese Endive Boats

Substitute 1½ (5.2-ounce) packages herb Boursin, at room temperature, for the blue cheese. Use only 5 to 5½ tablespoons milk and omit the pepper. Substitute 2 tablespoons minced fresh flat-leaf parsley for the chives.

oven-roasted caponata
with capers & raisins

bASICALLY AN ITALIAN RELATIVE OF RATATOUILLE because it's made with celery and olives, caponata is a quintessential ingredient of an antipasto platter. It's also great as a spread for toast or bread. Other interesting alternatives: Serve it in an omelette or make an Italian-style quesadilla of tortillas layered with caponata and Provolone.

2 medium (2 pounds) eggplants, cut into
  ¾-inch dice

½ cup olive oil, preferably extra-virgin

¼ teaspoon salt, or to taste

3 small red onions, thinly sliced

8 ripe (about 1½ pounds) small tomatoes,
  peeled, seeded, and chopped

1 cup brine-cured green and/or black olives,
  pitted and chopped

3 tablespoons drained capers

3 tablespoons golden raisins

¼ teaspoon freshly ground pepper, or to taste

4 celery stalks (including leaves), cut crosswise
  into thin slices

⅓ cup red wine vinegar

2 teaspoons sugar

¼ cup chopped fresh parsley, preferably flat-leaf

1. Preheat the oven to 500°F.

2. Spread the diced eggplant on two large baking sheets. Drizzle with ¼ cup of the oil, season with the salt, and toss to coat. Roast the eggplant for 10 minutes, stir with a wide spatula, and roast for 5 to 10 minutes longer, until dark golden brown. Set aside.

3. In a large skillet with a lid, heat the remaining ¼ cup oil over medium heat until hot but not smoking. Add the onions and cook, stirring, for 10 minutes, or until they are very soft but not browned. Add the tomatoes, olives, capers, raisins, and pepper, and simmer, covered, for 15 minutes.

4. Add the eggplant and celery to the skillet and cook over medium heat, stirring, for 10 minutes, or until the celery has softened. Stir in the vinegar and the sugar and cook for 5 minutes, or until the vinegar has evaporated. Remove from the heat and let cool.

5. Transfer the mixture to a platter and sprinkle with parsley. Serve at room temperature.

Serves 8

grilled jerk
chicken wings

WHEN GUESTS ARE EXPECTED FOR A MIDDAY cookout, start this appetizer the night before. The longer it marinates, the tastier it is.

10 scallions (white and tender green parts), chopped

4 jalapeño chiles, seeded and chopped

5 bay leaves, crumbled

2 tablespoons apple cider vinegar

4 garlic cloves, slivered

1 tablespoon ground allspice

2 teaspoons dried thyme

1¼ teaspoons salt

¾ teaspoon freshly ground pepper

5 pounds chicken wings, tips discarded and wings separated at the joint

1. Preheat the grill to medium-high and oil the rack.

2. In the bowl of a food processor, combine the scallions, jalapeños, bay leaves, vinegar, garlic, allspice, thyme, salt, and pepper and process until smooth.

3. In a large bowl, toss the chicken wings with the scallion mixture. Let the chicken stand at room temperature, turning frequently, for 20 minutes (or refrigerate, covered, overnight).

4. Grill the wings, in batches if necessary, turning with tongs, for about 10 minutes, or until cooked through.

Serves 8

spicy sirloin
satay

fOR INDONESIANS, SATAY IS EVERYDAY street food, easy to eat off bamboo skewers. Once you taste these, you may want them every day, too.

2 small scallions (white and tender green parts), coarsely chopped

2 small garlic cloves, coarsely chopped

1½ teaspoons minced peeled fresh ginger

1 jalapeño chile, coarsely chopped

1 teaspoon brown sugar

½ cup crunchy peanut butter

2 teaspoons soy sauce

1½ pounds boneless sirloin or other steak

Olive oil, for grilling

Salt and freshly ground pepper

1. Preheat the grill to high. Combine the scallions, garlic, ginger, jalapeño, sugar, peanut butter, and soy sauce in a blender. Add ½ cup hot water, ¼ cup at a time, and blend to a smooth paste, scraping down the sides.

2. Cut the steak into 2- by 1½- by ¼-inch-thick strips. Thread each onto a bamboo skewer; drizzle with olive oil, turning to coat. Season to taste with salt and pepper.

3. Grill the steak, turning once, until browned on both sides but still medium-rare, about 1½ minutes per side. Serve immediately, with the peanut sauce for dipping.

Serves 8

silver-dollar
crab cakes

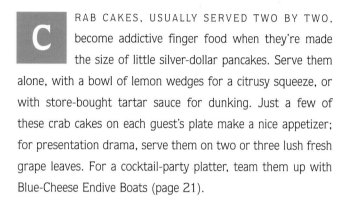

CRAB CAKES, USUALLY SERVED TWO BY TWO, become addictive finger food when they're made the size of little silver-dollar pancakes. Serve them alone, with a bowl of lemon wedges for a citrusy squeeze, or with store-bought tartar sauce for dunking. Just a few of these crab cakes on each guest's plate make a nice appetizer; for presentation drama, serve them on two or three lush fresh grape leaves. For a cocktail-party platter, team them up with Blue-Cheese Endive Boats (page 21).

I pound lump crabmeat, picked over to
remove any cartilage
3 tablespoons mayonnaise
2 tablespoons sour cream
I tablespoon whole-grain mustard
I large egg, lightly beaten
¼ teaspoon salt
¼ teaspoon freshly ground pepper
Lemon wedges, for serving

1. Preheat the oven to 400°F. Lightly butter one large or two small baking sheets.

2. In a medium bowl, using a fork, stir together the crab, mayonnaise, sour cream, mustard, egg, salt, and pepper until well combined.

3. Using a scant 1 tablespoon of the mixture per crab cake, form ½-inch-thick patties that are 1½ inches in diameter,

pressing them to hold together. As you shape the patties, arrange them, not quite touching, on the baking sheet(s).

4. Bake the crab cakes for 15 to 20 minutes, until golden brown. Let stand on the baking sheet(s) for 2 minutes. With a metal spatula, transfer the crab cakes to a platter. Serve warm with the lemon wedges.

Serves 8

spicy pasta
with cherry tomatoes

KICK OFF A LONG WEEKEND BY WHIPPING UP this quick pasta appetizer on a Friday evening, or serve it at the end of the weekend, as the first course of a languid Sunday supper. For young children, leave out the jalapeños, *por favor*. If you're not a cilantro fan, try using basil instead. Although those new "grape" tomatoes are delicious, their skins are too thick for this sauce; stick with regular cherry tomatoes.

I pound fusilli or bow-tie pasta

5 tablespoons unsalted butter

I to 3 jalapeño chiles, seeded if desired, and
   finely minced

6 cups (about 4 pints) cherry tomatoes, quartered

I teaspoon salt

Freshly ground pepper, to taste

½ cup chopped fresh cilantro

Freshly grated Parmesan cheese, for serving

1. In a large pot of boiling salted water, cook the pasta until it is al dente.

2. Meanwhile, melt the butter in a large deep skillet over medium-high heat. Add the jalapeños and cook, stirring, until they are slightly softened, 1 to 2 minutes. Add the tomatoes, salt, and pepper; reduce the heat to medium. Cook the mixture, stirring occasionally, until the tomatoes are slightly softened and very juicy. Stir in the cilantro, remove from the heat, and set aside.

3. Drain the pasta, reserving ½ cup of the pasta cooking water, and return the pasta to the pot. Add the tomato sauce and heat over low heat, stirring occasionally, for 1 to 2 minutes to allow the pasta to absorb some of the sauce; if the pasta seems dry, add some of the reserved pasta water.

4. Transfer the pasta to a serving bowl or divide among individual dinner plates. Serve immediately, passing the Parmesan cheese at the table.

Serves 8

adobo shrimp
pick-up sticks

aDOBO IS A SPICY MEXICAN FLAVORING PASTE or sauce, used in a wide variety of dishes; here we treat it as a marinade for shrimp. Packaged dried ancho chiles are available in many supermarkets and in specialty markets. Anchos are dark red and somewhat rounded; they are sometimes mistakenly marked pasillas, which are thinner and dark brown.

ADOBO MARINADE

3 large dried ancho chiles

2 garlic cloves, crushed

⅛ teaspoon dried oregano

⅛ teaspoon ground cumin

Generous pinch of ground coriander

Pinch of ground cinnamon

Pinch of ground cloves

1½ teaspoons salt

2 tablespoons white vinegar

2 tablespoons vegetable oil

1¼ to 1½ pounds medium shrimp,
    peeled and deveined

1. Make the adobo marinade: Heat a dry heavy medium skillet over medium heat. Add the chiles and toast them, pressing on them with a wooden spoon and turning them occasionally, until they are slightly softened and beginning to darken. Let cool.

2. Tear the chiles in half and discard the seeds. Put the chiles in a small bowl, add hot water to cover by about 1 inch, and let soak until softened, about 30 minutes (put a small saucer on top of the chiles if necessary to keep them submerged).

3. Remove the chiles from the water and set the water aside. Remove and discard the stems and tear the chiles into 1-inch pieces. In a blender, combine the chiles, garlic, oregano, cumin, coriander, cinnamon, cloves, salt, vinegar, and oil. Add 2 tablespoons of the reserved chile water and process the mixture until pureed, stopping frequently to scrape down the sides of the container with a rubber spatula and adding a bit more of the chile water if necessary. The marinade can be made up to 2 days ahead.

4. In a large bowl, combine the shrimp and enough of the marinade to coat generously. Any remaining marinade can be refrigerated for up to 5 days for another use, such as grilling chicken. Cover the shrimp and refrigerate for at least 30 minutes and up to 2 hours.

5. Preheat the grill to medium. If you are using wooden skewers, soak them in warm water for 15 minutes; drain.

6. Starting with the tail end, thread 1 shrimp lengthwise onto each skewer. Oil the grill rack. Grill the shrimp, turning once, until they are pink and just opaque throughout, 2 to 3 minutes per side. Serve hot on the skewers.

Serves 8

farm-fresh
creamy corn soup

ORN CONNOISSEURS BELIEVE YOU SHOULD already have your water boiling as you bring ears home from the farm stand—it's that much better fresh. They also say that Fourth of July marks the official start of corn season. The pure-corn version of this soup is fabulous, but you can make the corn-and-tomato variation if the tomatoes at the farm stand look especially tempting.

8 large ears corn, husked

3 tablespoons unsalted butter

3 garlic cloves, finely chopped

Two 14¼-ounce cans low-sodium chicken broth

¾ teaspoon salt, or more to taste

Freshly ground pepper, to taste

1 cup half-and-half

3 scallions (white and tender green parts), minced

1. Cut the kernels from the corn; set aside.

2. In a large heavy pot, melt the butter over medium heat. Add the garlic and cook, stirring, until softened, 1 to 2 minutes. Add the broth, salt, and pepper, stir well, and bring to a simmer, stirring occasionally. Simmer gently, stirring occasionally, for 5 minutes to blend the flavors.

3. Add the corn, increase the heat to medium-high, and bring to a gentle boil. Cook, stirring occasionally, until the corn kernels are tender, 5 to 7 minutes. Remove from the heat. Transfer about 1 cup of the soup to a blender and puree.

Return the puree to the soup. Stir in the half-and-half and bring just to a simmer. Season to taste with salt and pepper and remove from the heat.

4. Ladle the soup into bowls, sprinkle with scallions, and serve.

Serves 8

Fresh Corn & Tomato Soup

Add 2 ripe medium tomatoes, halved, seeded, and diced, to the soup along with the corn kernels.

cold cucumber soup
with yogurt & mint

WHEN YOU BEGIN A MEAL WITH THIS REFRESHing soup, guests always have room for more. It's a nice prelude to Tandoori-Marinated Butterflied Leg of Lamb (page 96). Or if you're really in a time bind, just make the soup and follow up with spicy Indian takeout. Feel free to substitute dill for the mint garnish. Poured from a jumbo Thermos, this soup adds a surprising elegance to a picnic.

APPETIZERS

4 large cucumbers

1½ cups chicken stock or canned low-sodium broth

2 garlic cloves, very finely minced

1½ cups plain low-fat yogurt

¾ teaspoon salt, or to taste

Freshly ground white or black pepper to taste

1 bunch mint, leaves only, finely slivered

1. Peel the cucumbers and cut them lengthwise in half. Scoop out the seeds with a teaspoon or a melon baller and discard. Cut the cucumbers into 1-inch chunks.

2. Combine half the cucumbers and ¼ cup of the stock in a food processor and process, scraping down the sides of the bowl a few times, until the cucumbers are very finely chopped. Transfer to a large bowl. Repeat with the remaining cucumbers and another ¼ cup of the stock.

3. Add the garlic and yogurt to the cucumbers and stir until well blended. Stir in the remaining 1 cup stock, the salt, and

pepper. Cover and refrigerate for 1 to 2 hours, until cold. (The soup can be made up to 1 day ahead.)

4. Just before serving, season the soup with salt and pepper if needed. Ladle into shallow bowls and garnish each serving with a sprinkling of mint.

Serves 8

Movable Feasts

Vintage trays gather dust in secondhand shops and hide in boxes at yard sales, but they are versatile collectibles that instantly make a party portable. There is no shortage of metal cocktail trays from the forties through the sixties, many printed with recipes for drinks or with repeat motifs like clocks and roosters. Mini promotional trays from the past, given out at tourist stops like motels and gas stations, feature lithographed scenes and vistas; their diminutive size is perfect for transporting little bites from kitchen to outdoor table. Humble old wooden trays are another option. Make wooden trays your own by painting them with oil-based paint or by decoupaging them.

chapter two
salads & side dishes

caesar salad
with chili croutons

WHEN MEMORIAL DAY SNEAKS UP ON YOU AND suddenly you're in the thick of summer, you'll appreciate this easy but crowd-pleasing salad. Caesar salad was actually first served in Tijuana, Mexico, not in Italy, as many people think. So here we dusted the croutons with chili powder for a Southwestern accent. If you make the croutons and dressing beforehand, all you need to do is toss the greens together at the last minute.

CHILI CROUTONS

One 1-pound loaf sourdough or country-style
    bread, cut into ½-inch cubes

1 tablespoon vegetable oil

½ to 1 teaspoon chili powder

CAESAR SALAD

3 tablespoons fresh lemon juice

2 garlic cloves, minced

¾ cup plus 2 tablespoons freshly grated
    Parmesan cheese

½ teaspoon anchovy paste

½ teaspoon Dijon mustard

⅜ teaspoon salt, or to taste

¼ teaspoon freshly ground pepper, or to taste

½ cup olive oil

2 heads romaine lettuce, trimmed,
    quartered lengthwise, and cut crosswise
    into ½-inch-wide strips

1. Preheat the oven to 325°F.

2. Make the chili croutons: In a large bowl, toss the bread cubes with the vegetable oil, then sprinkle with the chili powder. Spread on a large baking sheet and toast in the oven, stirring once or twice, for 12 to 15 minutes, until crisp and lightly browned. Let cool. The croutons can be made 2 days ahead and stored in an airtight container at room temperature.

3. Make the Caesar salad: Combine the lemon juice, garlic, ¼ cup plus 2 tablespoons of the Parmesan, the anchovy paste, mustard, salt, and pepper in a blender and blend until smooth. With the blender running, add the olive oil in a slow, steady stream, blending until the dressing is thick and smooth. The dressing can be made up to 1 day ahead and kept, covered, in the refrigerator.

4. In a large bowl, combine the lettuce and croutons. Add the dressing, tossing to coat. Add the remaining ½ cup Parmesan, tossing to coat. Serve immediately.

Serves 8

zesty
carrot salad

W E SAVED SO MUCH TIME BY USING PREPARED julienne carrots from the market, we had a few extra minutes to play with the presentation: Mix the entire salad in a bowl, then transfer it into a clean vintage lunch box or picnic tin for a boxed lunch appearance. This sweet and sour and spicy salad adds color to any picnic or buffet.

One 10-ounce package julienne carrots

⅓ cup fresh cilantro leaves

2 tablespoons seasoned rice vinegar

2 teaspoons fresh lime juice

1½ teaspoons Asian (toasted) sesame oil

¼ teaspoon salt

⅛ teaspoon ground red pepper

⅛ teaspoon finely grated lime zest

In a medium bowl, stir together all the ingredients. Serve immediately or refrigerate, covered, until ready to serve.

Serves 4 to 6

■ Note

If you make this recipe starting with whole carrots, you'll need to do some chopping. Julienne, also called matchsticks, are long strips about ⅛ inch thick. For carrots, peel them first, then cut each carrot crosswise into pieces about 2 inches long and square off their sides. Cut the pieces lengthwise into thin slices and then into long thin strips, each about ⅛ inch thick.

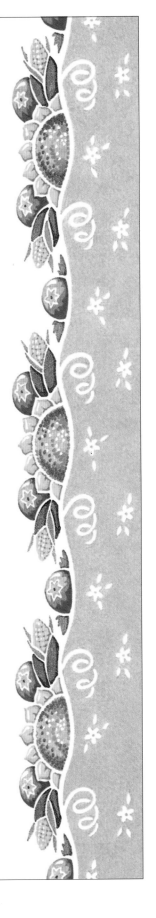

coleslaw
asian style

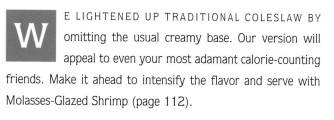

W E LIGHTENED UP TRADITIONAL COLESLAW BY omitting the usual creamy base. Our version will appeal to even your most adamant calorie-counting friends. Make it ahead to intensify the flavor and serve with Molasses-Glazed Shrimp (page 112).

4 cups finely shredded red cabbage

1 teaspoon salt

½ cup rice vinegar

½ cup sugar

1 tablespoon minced peeled fresh ginger

½ teaspoon crushed red pepper flakes

3 medium carrots, peeled and finely shredded

1 tablespoon finely chopped fresh cilantro

1. In a large colander, toss the cabbage with the salt. Top the cabbage with a plate, weight the plate with a 1-pound can, and let drain in the sink for at least 1 hour and up to 3 hours. Rinse and drain the cabbage completely.

2. In a large bowl, whisk together the rice vinegar, sugar, ginger, and pepper flakes until the sugar has dissolved. Add the cabbage and carrots and toss to combine well. Store refrigerated, covered, stirring occasionally, until very cold.

3. In the colander, drain the slaw. Taste and adjust the seasonings, especially the salt. Transfer to a serving bowl and garnish with the cilantro.

Serves 6

mint & olive
fennel toss

i T'S MUGGY OUT AND ALL YOU WANT IS SOMEthing cool and crisp: Here's your ticket, a brisk duet of mint and fennel. This dish is beautiful, and healthful, presented on a bed of baby spinach; use one cup per person.

2 large fennel bulbs, trimmed and sliced lengthwise into 3 x ¾-inch lengthwise strips, plus

1 tablespoon minced fennel fronds, if available

¾ cup finely chopped red onion

⅓ cup finely chopped fresh mint

2 tablespoons finely chopped pitted Mediterranean green olives

2 teaspoons grated lemon zest

2 tablespoons fresh lemon juice

1 tablespoon olive oil

¼ teaspoon salt

⅛ teaspoon freshly ground pepper

1. In a medium bowl, stir together the fennel and fennel fronds, red onion, mint, olives, lemon zest, olive oil, lemon juice, salt, and pepper.

2. Let the salad stand at room temperature until ready to serve, up to 3 hours.

Serves 4

SALADS &
SIDE DISHES

cantaloupe
ambrosia

WITH ITS TROPICAL GOOD LOOKS AND TASTE, this sorbet-hued salad is great for a pool party. Mound it in a glass bowl nestled in a larger glass bowl of ice. You can substitute any melon you like—Persian, honeydew, and casaba are all fine choices. Remember: The key to choosing a ripe melon is to feel for a slight softness (not mushiness) and sniff a full fruity fragrance.

One 3½-ounce can sweetened flaked coconut

¾ cup boiling water

¼ teaspoon grated lime zest

4 cups cantaloupe balls, chilled

1. In a blender, puree the coconut with the water and the zest for about 1 minute on high speed. Let the mixture stand for 10 minutes. Press it through a fine strainer set over a bowl. Let the coconut milk come to room temperature, then chill, covered, until very cold.

2. Transfer the cantaloupe to a serving bowl, add the coconut milk, and serve immediately.

Serves 4 to 6

greek
beet salad

HERE'S A SALAD THAT'S PERFECT TO BRING along on a picnic: no wilted greens to worry about. A classic in Greece, the apple-beet combo's pure flavors complement the smokiness of any grilled fare, such as Grilled Pork Chops on Arugula Salad (page 100) or Rosemary & Garlic Lamb Chops (page 94). Choose eating apples only, namely good old Red Delicious (the flesh doesn't darken as quickly as that of other apples), glorious Granny Smith (the tartness makes a nice counterpoint to the sweet beets), or tangy, juicy Winesap.

⅓ cup plain yogurt

1 tablespoon drained capers, minced

¼ teaspoon salt, or to taste

Freshly ground pepper, to taste

Two 15-ounce cans sliced beets, drained

2 small apples, peeled, cored, and cut
    into thin wedges

1. In a medium bowl, stir the yogurt, capers, salt, and pepper together.

2. Stir in the beets and apples. Serve immediately at room temperature or chill, covered with plastic wrap, for several hours before serving cold.

Serves 4 to 6

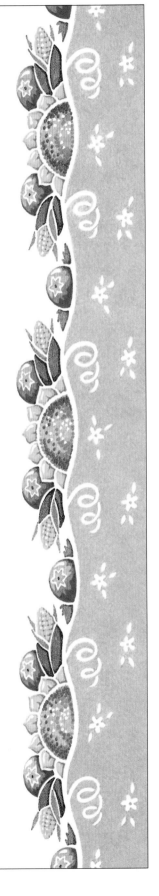

tomato feast
with feta & olives

tOMATOES OF ALL SHAPES AND SIZES, FROM tiny Sun Golds to big-as-a-baseball Brandywines, can all find a place in this salad. So time the meal for August or September, when gardens fairly drip with tomatoes and local farm stands overflow. Labor Day weekend would be ideal. Here we make a fragrant basil-flavored oil with olive oil—use the best you can find.

FRESH BASIL OIL
½ cup lightly packed fresh basil leaves
¼ cup olive oil
Salt, to taste

2 pounds assorted ripe tomatoes, cut into
 ¼-inch-thick slices
2 cups cherry, grape, and/or other small tomatoes
Salt and freshly ground pepper
3 ounces feta cheese
½ cup good-quality black olives, pitted
Fresh basil leaves, for garnish

1. Make the fresh basil oil: Bring a medium pot of salted water to a boil. Put the basil leaves in a small strainer and immerse the strainer in the boiling water just until the basil is wilted, 10 to 15 seconds. Rinse under cold water until cooled, then drain well on paper towels. Squeeze the basil dry, then wrap in dry paper towels and squeeze out any remaining moisture.

2. Put the basil in a blender, add the oil and salt, and process until pureed. The basil oil can be made 1 day ahead, covered, and refrigerated. Bring to room temperature before using.

3. Arrange the sliced tomatoes on a large platter and scatter the cherry tomatoes over them. Sprinkle with salt and a generous amount of pepper to taste. Crumble the feta over the tomatoes, scatter the olives over, and spoon the basil oil over all. Garnish with a few basil leaves and serve immediately.

Serves 8

Flavored Oils

Because they pack a punch, use flavored oils sparingly. To make them: Warm oil over low heat until fragrant, about 5 minutes. Pour into glass jars, add ingredients, seal, and let steep 1 hour. Store, refrigerated, for up to 3 days. Try:

• oregano, thyme, and olive oil

• chervil, tarragon, shallots, and peanut oil

• fresh ginger, cardamom seed, coriander leaf, and safflower oil

• dill and sunflower oil

• lemon verbena, lemon thyme, and walnut oil

warm grilled salad
of red onion & tomato

SALADS &
SIDE DISHES

BECAUSE THEY'RE MEATIER AND LESS JUICY than round tomatoes, egg-shaped plum tomatoes hold their own on the grill without falling apart. Think of this recipe as either a hearty warm salad or a side dish for grilled meat or chicken. It is a superb complement to Tandoori-Marinated Butterflied Leg of Lamb (page 96).

3 small to medium red onions, cut into
  ½-inch-thick rounds
8 small to medium plum tomatoes, halved lengthwise
Olive oil, for brushing
Salt and freshly ground pepper
⅓ cup packed slivered fresh basil

1. Preheat the grill to medium-high.

2. If desired, secure each onion round with a toothpick or a small skewer; this will help keep them from separating when they are turned on the grill. Lightly brush the onions on both sides with oil and season with salt and pepper. Lightly brush the cut sides of the tomatoes with oil and season with salt and pepper.

3. Place the onions on the grill and place the tomatoes, cut side down, next to them. Grill the onions, turning once, until they are lightly charred and beginning to soften, 4 to 6 minutes on each side. Grill the tomatoes, turning them once, until they are lightly charred on the cut sides and beginning to soften, 2 to 3 minutes per side.

4. Arrange the tomatoes cut side up on a serving platter. Remove the toothpicks from the onions if you used them, separate the onions into rings, and scatter them over the tomatoes. Sprinkle the basil over the top and serve warm or at room temperature.

Serves 8

balsamic-dressed
zucchini slices

W E SEE YOU ENJOYING THIS DISH ON A SUNSET cruise with a basket of fried chicken (takeout is okay), a bottle of dry, crisp rosé, and perhaps a few brownies for dessert. It's fast and easy to prepare—and can be made ahead: You just fry up the zucchini and let it sit in a marinade for up to three days. Bon voyage!

3 tablespoons balsamic vinegar

3 tablespoons golden raisins

1 tablespoon minced fresh mint, plus fresh mint

   sprigs, for garnish

1 teaspoon dark brown sugar

1 garlic clove, halved

½ teaspoon salt, or to taste

⅛ teaspoon freshly ground pepper, or to taste

Vegetable oil, for frying

8 small zucchini (about 5 ounces each), cut

   crosswise into ¼-inch-thick slices

1 tablespoon pine nuts, toasted

1. In a large bowl, stir the vinegar, raisins, mint, sugar, garlic, salt, and pepper together. Set the mixture aside.

2. In a large skillet, heat about ½ inch of oil over medium-high heat until hot but not smoking. Add about 2 cups of the zucchini slices to the oil and fry, stirring occasionally, for 7 to 10 minutes, until golden brown. With a slotted spoon, transfer the cooked zucchini to a strainer set over a bowl to drain. While still hot, add the zucchini to the vinegar mixture, stirring to coat. Repeat with the remaining zucchini in batches of about 2 cups each. Add more oil to the skillet as necessary.

3. Let the mixture stand at room temperature for at least 1 hour before serving, or chill, covered, for up to 3 days.

4. Serve the zucchini at room temperature, topped with the pine nuts and garnished with mint sprigs.

Serves 4 to 6

country supper
corn pudding

SALADS &
SIDE DISHES

fRESH CORN AND SUMMER HERBS BAKE into a sweet and delicate creamy custard. Prepare the corn and other ingredients early in the day, cover, and refrigerate separately; then just mix up the pudding shortly before dinner and slip it into the oven while you head out to the grill.

in this water bath keeps the texture creamy.) Bake for 25 to 30 minutes, until the custard is just set. Serve immediately.

Serves 8

6 large ears corn, husked and kernels removed

1½ cups half-and-half

3 large eggs, beaten

2 tablespoons unsalted butter, melted

¼ cup finely chopped fresh basil

2 tablespoons finely chopped fresh chives

1 teaspoon salt, or more to taste

¼ teaspoon freshly ground pepper

1. Preheat the oven to 350°F. Lightly butter a 13- by 9-inch baking dish or shallow 2-quart baking dish.

2. In the bowl of a food processor, process ½ cup of the corn kernels to a coarse puree. Transfer to a large bowl and add the remaining corn, the half-and-half, eggs, melted butter, basil, chives, salt, and pepper, stirring until well blended. Pour the mixture into the prepared baking dish, making sure the corn is evenly distributed.

3. Set the baking dish in a larger baking pan, place in the oven, and add enough hot water to the baking pan to come about halfway up the sides of the baking dish. (Baking the pudding

Salad Days

Greens taste great with these easy dressings kids can make. Combine ingredients in a jar and let the kids shake it to their hearts' content.

Festive French: ⅓ cup olive oil; ¼ cup ketchup; ¼ cup mayonnaise; 3 tablespoons apple cider vinegar; 1 teaspoon sugar; ½ teaspoon paprika; and salt and pepper to taste

Green Goddess Garlic: ½ cup mayonnaise; ½ cup sour cream; 1 tablespoon apple cider vinegar; ½ cup chopped fresh parsley; 1 tablespoon chopped scallions; 1 garlic clove, minced; a dollop of Dijon mustard; and salt and white pepper to taste

Instant Italian: ½ cup olive oil; ½ cup red wine vinegar; 3 garlic cloves, minced; 1 tablespoon each chopped fresh basil and oregano; and salt and pepper to taste

grilled corn on the cob

WHEN IT'S GRILLED IN ITS HUSK, CORN HAS A sweetness that seems to intensify. To gauge if it's ready, don't hesitate to peek inside the husk—there should be little brown spots all over. Rather than slathering on butter and salt, try miso or a light oil-and-vinegar dressing.

> **3 tablespoons butter, at room temperature**
>
> **1 small shallot, finely chopped**
>
> **2 tablespoons minced fresh parsley**
>
> **½ teaspoon grated lemon zest**
>
> **½ teaspoon salt**
>
> **⅛ teaspoon freshly ground pepper**
>
> **6 ears fresh corn, with husks**

1. Preheat the grill to medium-high.

2. In a small bowl, stir together the butter, shallot, parsley, lemon zest, salt, and pepper. Let stand at room temperature.

3. Pull the husks back on each ear of corn, leaving them attached at the stalk end; remove the silks. In a large pot, soak the corn in water to cover for at least 10 minutes. Drain.

4. Brush the kernels of each ear of corn with the butter mixture. Pull the husks back up over the kernels and tie them together at the top with string.

5. Grill the corn, turning frequently, for 15 to 20 minutes, until the husks are dry and the kernels are beginning to brown.

Serves 6

summery corn saute

INSTEAD OF PAIRING CORN WITH LIMA BEANS, we've combined summer's most sought-after vegetable with splashier bell pepper and zucchini for color and crunch. It's fine to substitute olive oil for butter, basil for cilantro. This works with just about any grilled entree.

> **3 tablespoons unsalted butter**
>
> **2 garlic cloves, minced**
>
> **1 red bell pepper, cored, seeded, and cut into ¼-inch dice**
>
> **2 zucchini, cut into ¼-inch dice**
>
> **4 cups (6 to 8 ears) corn kernels**
>
> **1 teaspoon salt, or more to taste**
>
> **¼ teaspoon freshly ground pepper**
>
> **4 scallions (white and tender green parts), minced**
>
> **3 tablespoons finely chopped fresh cilantro**

1. In a large deep skillet, melt the butter over medium-high heat. Add the garlic and cook, stirring, just until fragrant, about 30 seconds. Add the bell pepper and cook, stirring, until it starts to soften, about 2 minutes. Stir in the zucchini and saute until it is slightly softened, 3 to 4 minutes.

2. Add the corn, salt, and pepper and cook, stirring, just until the corn is crisp-tender, 3 to 4 minutes. Stir in the scallions and cilantro and cook, stirring once or twice, just until the scallions are starting to wilt, about 1 minute longer. Serve immediately.

Serves 8

grilled corn &
tomato jamboree

C OMBINED WITH JUICY RIPE TOMATOES, scallions, and lots of fresh herbs, smoky-sweet grilled corn makes a delicious height-of-the-summer salad. But don't discard those cobs! When they are dried, toss them into the grill fire to enhance and sweeten the flavors of beef or pork.

MUSTARD VINAIGRETTE

3 tablespoons olive oil

1 tablespoon white wine vinegar

¼ teaspoon Dijon mustard

¾ teaspoon salt, or to taste

Freshly ground pepper, to taste

8 ears corn, husked

4 ripe tomatoes, cut into ¼-inch dice

1 bunch scallions (white and tender green parts),
    thinly sliced

¼ cup packed chopped mixed fresh herbs,
    such as basil, flat-leaf parsley, and tarragon,
    plus herb sprigs for garnish

Arugula, for garnish

1. Preheat the grill to high.

2. Make the mustard vinaigrette: In a jar, combine the oil, vinegar, mustard, salt, and pepper. Cover and shake to blend well; set aside.

3. Grill the corn, turning frequently, until slightly charred all over, 3 to 5 minutes. Let cool slightly, then, with a sharp knife, slice the kernels from the cobs (cutting the cobs in half makes this easier). Transfer the corn to a large bowl.

4. Add the tomatoes, scallions, and chopped herbs to the corn and toss to mix well. Add the dressing and toss again. Transfer to a serving dish and garnish with herb sprigs and arugula. Serve at room temperature.

Serves 8

IF YOU PRAY FOR RAIN, BE PREPARED TO DEAL WITH SOME MUD.

garlic-buttered
crispy potatoes

I F YOU'RE HAVING THAT MEAT-AND-POTATOES crowd for dinner but still want to do something special, this dish fits the bill. You can partially cook the potatoes beforehand, then grill them just before serving. They look pretty sprinkled with finely chopped basil or chives.

**2½ pounds small Yukon Gold or other waxy potatoes
(1½ to 2 inches in diameter), halved crosswise**

4 tablespoons (½ stick) unsalted butter

2 to 3 garlic cloves, smashed

Salt and freshly ground pepper

1. Cook the potatoes in a large pot of boiling salted water until just tender but still firm, 8 to 10 minutes. Drain and set aside. (The potatoes can be cooked early in the day and kept, loosely covered, in the refrigerator; bring them to room temperature before proceeding.)

2. Preheat the grill to high. Soak 8 to 16 long bamboo skewers in water while the grill heats.

3. Meanwhile, combine the butter and garlic in a small heavy skillet and heat over very low heat, stirring once or twice and mashing the garlic cloves to release their flavor, until the butter becomes fragrant and the garlic is barely starting to color. Remove the skillet from the heat and discard the garlic; keep the butter warm.

4. Thread the potatoes onto the skewers, skewering the halves crosswise so that the cut sides face out. Place the skewers on a platter, brush the potatoes generously on all sides with the garlic butter, and sprinkle with salt and pepper. Grill the potatoes, turning frequently and brushing several times with the remaining butter, until golden brown and crisp, 5 to 7 minutes. Return the skewers to the platter, turning to coat with any remaining butter, and serve immediately.

Serves 8

Beat the Clock

When you're rushed with last-minute preparations, do you really want to stop and chop? Here are some tips that help clear the road:

- Keep toasted almonds on hand to sprinkle on salads or grilled fish. Place them one layer deep on a baking sheet in a 350°F oven and toast for 10 minutes, or until golden. Store at room temperature in a sealed container for up to 1 month.

- When a recipe calls for garlic, reach for your premade garlic puree. Mince cloves in a food processor, transfer to a small jar, stir in a tablespoon of olive oil, and store in the refrigerator for up to 3 days.

warm potato salad
with bacon curls

WARM POTATO SALAD WITH BACON: LOOK UP "comfort food" in the dictionary and this is what you might find. An essential part of every picnic and barbecue, potato salad is as American as apple pie. When your cousin, the Low-Fat Queen, isn't looking, feel free to add a tablespoon or so of bacon drippings to the dressing for extra-heavenly flavor. For this salad, choose potatoes of similar size so they cook evenly. Since the dish can be served at room temperature, it is a convenient choice for a buffet.

3 pounds red-skinned or other waxy potatoes

6 to 8 slices bacon, cut crosswise into
   ½-inch-wide strips

MUSTARD DRESSING

½ cup olive oil

¼ cup white wine vinegar

2 tablespoons Dijon mustard

½ teaspoon salt, or more to taste

Freshly ground pepper, to taste

4 scallions (white and tender green parts),
   thinly sliced

¼ cup chopped fresh parsley

1. Put the potatoes in a large pot, add salted water to cover by about 1 inch, and bring to a boil. Reduce heat and cook at a gentle boil just until the potatoes are tender when pierced with a knife, 15 to 20 minutes; do not overcook. Drain thoroughly.

2. Meanwhile, in a large skillet, cook the bacon over medium-low heat, stirring occasionally, until golden brown and crisp. With a slotted spoon, transfer to paper towels to drain.

3. Make the mustard dressing: In a small jar, combine the oil, vinegar, mustard, salt, and pepper. Seal tightly and shake to blend well. Set aside.

4. As soon as the potatoes are cool enough to handle, cut them into ½-inch chunks. In a large bowl, toss the warm potatoes with the dressing. Add the bacon, scallions, and parsley and toss well. Serve warm or at room temperature.

Serves 8

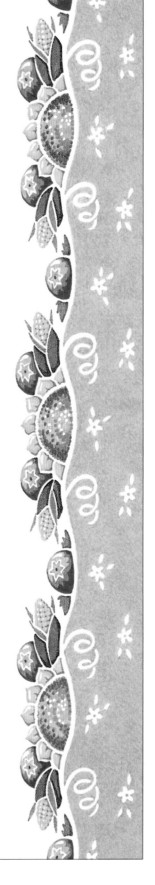

tzatziki
potato salad

i F YOU'VE EVER EATEN IN AN AUTHENTIC Greek restaurant, then you know that tzatziki, a sauce made of cucumber and yogurt, is a mealtime essential, both as a dip for pita bread and as a palate cleanser. Here, it adds tang to potato salad.

2 cups plain yogurt

1 English (seedless) cucumber, unpeeled, seeded
   and cut into 1/4-inch dice

Salt

2 tablespoons olive oil

2 tablespoons finely chopped fresh dill,
   plus additional sprigs for garnish

1 tablespoon red wine vinegar

1 garlic clove, chopped and mashed to a
   paste with 1/4 teaspoon salt

Freshly ground pepper, to taste

3 pounds little red-skinned potatoes, peeled and
   cut into 3/4-inch pieces

1. In a fine strainer set over a bowl, drain the yogurt for at least 2 hours at room temperature. Discard the liquid.

2. Meanwhile, in a colander, toss together the cucumber and 1 teaspoon salt and drain for at least 1 hour at room temperature. Wrap the cucumber in a clean dish towel and squeeze to remove as much liquid as possible. Pat the cucumber dry on paper towels or a clean dish towel.

3. In a large bowl, stir together the drained yogurt, the cucumber, the olive oil, chopped dill, vinegar, and garlic paste and season with salt and pepper. Let stand for 1 hour at room temperature.

4. In a steamer set over boiling water, steam the potatoes, covered, for 8 to 10 minutes, until they are tender when pierced with a fork. Transfer the potatoes to a bowl, season with salt and pepper, and let come to room temperature. Stir the potatoes into the tzatziki until combined well, and refrigerate, covered, until ready to serve. Serve cool or at room temperature, garnished with the dill sprigs.

Serves 8

canadian-bacon
sweet potato salad

dON'T RELEGATE YOUR SWEET POTATOES TO Thanksgiving! As Southerners well know, they're welcome guests at any summer meal. In this case, presented on a bed of greens, they bring an interesting twist to ordinary potato salad. Serve this salad for lunch or dinner.

2 pounds sweet potatoes, peeled and cut into ¾-inch cubes

½ cup mango chutney, large pieces chopped

6 scallions (white and tender green parts), finely chopped

¼ cup vegetable oil

1 tablespoon apple cider vinegar

¼ teaspoon salt

¼ teaspoon freshly ground pepper

One 6-ounce package sliced Canadian bacon, cut into ¼-inch-wide strips

¼ cup minced fresh cilantro

6 cups mixed greens such as mesclun, rinsed and spun dry

1. In a large pot, bring the sweet potatoes and enough salted cold water to cover to a boil. Cook for about 10 minutes, or until the potatoes are tender when pierced with a fork. Drain the sweet potatoes in a colander and return them to the pot. Shake the pan over high heat for 30 seconds, or until any excess liquid has evaporated. Remove the pan from the heat.

2. In a large bowl, whisk together the chutney, scallions, oil, vinegar, salt, and pepper until combined well.

3. Transfer the potatoes to the bowl with the chutney mixture. Stir in the Canadian bacon and cilantro. Serve the salad warm, at room temperature, or chilled, on the mixed greens.

Serves 6

cultivate an enchanted evening
potting-shed buffet

here's a way of giving an outdoor party a theme without having to scoot all over town buying decorations. Think tool shed and potting bench, and start gathering. Choose whatever contributes to the atmosphere. Don't fret over a little rust or mud here and there on items that won't touch food—it's all part of the look!

HOW DOES A GARDEN PARTY GROW?

zesty carrot salad
(page 31)

**tomato feast
with feta & olives**
(page 34)

three-berry couscous salad
(page 51)

b.l.t. pasta salad
(page 78)

**tandoori-marinated
butterflied leg of lamb**
(page 96)

mocha-bourbon mud cake
(page 124)

sweet ricotta & plum pizza
(page 134)

**Zinfandel or
Petite Sirah, iced tea,
and sparkling water**

Green-Thumb Tabletop

Ideally, all your supplies are around the house or shed. Here are a few possibilities:

- Use a potting table—or an old, rustic, worn door set on wood sawhorses—as your outdoor sideboard.

- Announce each dish from your menu by writing its name on a garden plant label; stand the labels in little terra-cotta pots filled with sand or potting soil.

- Turn a clean wheelbarrow into an ice trough.

- Mass some majolica: Basketweave and corn-motif bowls, strawberry-embossed platters, and plates shaped like begonia leaves will look right at home.

- Cluster several wire, glass, or ceramic flower frogs together. They make great holders for skewers, straws, and swizzle sticks.

- Create centerpieces with garden-related collectibles—weathered watering cans and vintage sprinklers, perhaps?

french
lentil salad

t HIS EASY BUT UNUSUAL LEGUME SALAD would be particularly good with Tandoori-Marinated Butterflied Leg of Lamb (page 96) or with grilled salmon. The small French lentils, sometimes called "lentilles le Puy," are available in gourmet markets and health food stores. They are delicious, and they also hold their shape after cooking, unlike other types—do not be tempted to substitute regular lentils, as they will fall apart. Chicken broth adds flavor, but you can use water instead for a vegetarian version.

Generous 2 cups (about 1 pound) small French
    lentils (lentilles le Puy), picked over and rinsed
¾ cup red lentils (about 6 ounces), picked
    over and rinsed
1 carrot, halved
1 onion, halved
One 14½-ounce can low-sodium chicken broth
3 tablespoons balsamic vinegar, or more to taste
4½ tablespoons olive oil
¼ cup plus 2 tablespoons finely chopped fresh
    flat-leaf parsley
Salt and freshly ground pepper

1. Put the French lentils in a large saucepan and add a half carrot, a half onion, half the chicken broth, and enough water to cover by 2 inches. Bring to a boil over high heat, reduce the heat, and simmer gently until just tender, 15 to 20 minutes. Drain the lentils and discard the carrot and onion.

2. Meanwhile, put the red lentils in a medium saucepan and add the remaining carrot, onion, broth, and enough water to cover by 2 inches. Bring to a boil over high heat, reduce the heat, and simmer gently until the lentils are tender and falling apart, 12 to 15 minutes. Drain and discard the carrot and onion.

3. Combine the lentils in a large bowl. Add the vinegar and then the oil, stirring gently with a rubber spatula to blend. Stir in the parsley and season to taste with salt and pepper. Serve warm or at room temperature. The salad can be made up to 1 day ahead and stored, covered, in the refrigerator; bring to room temperature before serving.

Serves 8

pasta salad
with jalapeños & feta

mEXICO MEETS GREECE IN THIS QUICK PASTA dish. South-of-the-border jalapeño chile combines with Mediterranean feta cheese, kalamata olives, and oregano to make a sunny meal that's easy whatever the weather—or season. By the time the pasta water boils, you'll be done whipping the other ingredients together.

1 pound penne pasta

1 small red onion, cut into rings

½ cup fresh flat-leaf parsley leaves

1 small fresh red or green jalapeño chile, seeded
   and coarsely chopped

2 garlic cloves, chopped

2 teaspoons drained capers

1 teaspoon fresh oregano leaves

⅓ cup olive oil

4 ounces feta cheese, coarsely crumbled

12 kalamata olives, pitted and finely chopped

Salt, to taste

1. In a large pot of boiling salted water, cook the pasta until it is al dente. Place the red onions in a colander, drain the pasta in it, and transfer the pasta and onions to a serving bowl.

2. Meanwhile, finely chop the parsley, jalapeño, garlic, capers, and oregano together. Transfer the mixture to the serving bowl with the pasta.

3. Add the oil, feta, and olives to the pasta and toss until combined well. Season to taste with salt. Serve warm or at room temperature.

Serves 4 to 6

Wines of Summer

It's hot and you're barefoot. Why should your wine be anything but casual? Somehow, it's easier to toss the rule book when you're fanning the flames of a grill. Here are a few ideas:

- Pastas love a Cabernet or young Merlot.

- For light meats and cold poultry, try dry rosés and Beaujolais—and, yes, it's okay to chill light reds in summer.

- A spicy, smoky, meaty meal right off the grill—steak or lamb, perhaps? Reach for a Zinfandel or Petite Sirah.

- Seafood steaks beg for a crisp, buttery Chardonnay, whereas shellfish is perfectly complemented by Sauvignon Blanc or Muscadet from France.

Resist the temptation to overchill wine—if it's icy cold, you won't be able to taste it.

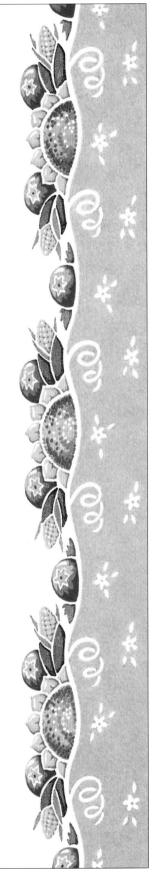

three-berry
couscous salad

tHIS SWEET-AND-SAVORY DISH, PERFECT WITH Pasta Salad with Jalapeños & Feta (page 49), could be made even healthier with whole-wheat couscous. This is the quintessential picnic food—easy and delicious.

I tablespoon vegetable oil

½ teaspoon salt

¼ teaspoon freshly ground pepper

⅛ teaspoon ground allspice

I cup couscous

2 scallions (white and tender green parts), trimmed and finely chopped

I pint small ripe strawberries, hulled and sliced

I cup small ripe blueberries, picked over

I cup small ripe raspberries, picked over

⅓ cup minced fresh parsley

2 tablespoons seasoned rice vinegar

1. In a large saucepan, bring 1½ cups water, the oil, salt, pepper, and allspice to a boil over high heat. Add the couscous and scallions and stir. Remove the pan from the heat and let stand, covered, for 5 minutes. Stir to fluff.

2. Transfer the warm couscous to a bowl and stir in the berries, parsley, and vinegar. Serve the salad warm or chilled.

Serves 6 to 8

portobellos
& arugula

pORTOBELLO MUSHROOMS ARE SO MEATY AND satisfying, they make a great alternative to steak. Try this with a crumble of goat cheese or a dab of melted mozzarella for even more flavor.

3 tablespoons olive oil

I shallot, finely chopped

I tablespoon red wine vinegar

¾ teaspoon whole-grain mustard

½ teaspoon fresh thyme

¼ teaspoon salt

Pinch of freshly ground pepper

4 medium portobello mushrooms (about 6 ounces), stems discarded

6 cups arugula, rinsed and spun dry

1. Preheat the grill to medium-high and oil the rack.

2. In a small bowl, whisk together the oil, shallot, vinegar, mustard, thyme, salt, and pepper. Set aside.

3. Grill the mushrooms, starting stem side down, for about 6 minutes on each side, until softened and cooked through.

4. Slice the warm mushrooms into thin strips. In a small bowl, toss with 2 tablespoons of well-stirred dressing. Toss the greens with the remaining dressing and arrange on 4 plates. Place the mushrooms in the center of the greens. Serve warm.

Serves 4

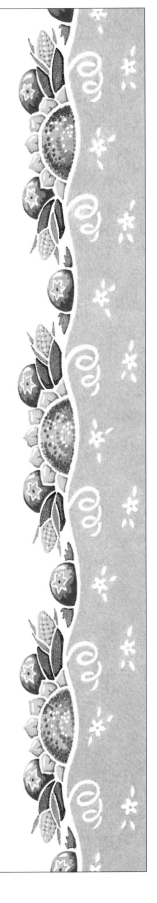

thai-style
beef salad

WE SEE THIS SALAD PRESENTED ON A TABLE SET with Thai silk runners and place mats and speckled coco wood chopsticks. A combination of fresh herbs, hot chile peppers, cooling lime juice, and tender slices of grilled beef, this dish tastes as good as it looks. Just before serving, garnish with cut limes and sprigs of cilantro or mint.

SPICY LIME DRESSING

2 to 4 jalapeño chiles, finely minced

3 garlic cloves, minced

½ cup freshly squeezed lime juice (about 4 limes)

2 teaspoons fish sauce (see Note)

2 teaspoons sugar

Salt, to taste

BEEF SALAD

2 to 2½ pounds boneless beef sirloin, about 1 inch thick

Salt and freshly ground black pepper

1 small red onion, halved lengthwise and thinly sliced crosswise

2 kirby (pickling) cucumbers or ½ English (seedless) cucumber, peeled, halved lengthwise, and thinly sliced crosswise

1 cup chopped fresh cilantro

⅔ cup packed slivered fresh mint

2 heads romaine or butter lettuce, cut crosswise into thin ribbons

1. Preheat the grill to medium-high.

2. Meanwhile, make the spicy lime dressing: In a small bowl, combine all the ingredients, stirring well to dissolve the sugar. Set the mixture aside.

3. Season the steak with salt and a generous amount of pepper. Grill, turning once, for 8 to 10 minutes for medium-rare, or to the desired doneness. Transfer to a cutting board and let rest for 5 minutes.

4. Cut the steak against the grain into thin slices. Transfer to a bowl, add the onion, cucumbers, cilantro, and mint, and toss to mix. Add the dressing and toss to coat. Arrange the lettuce on individual serving plates, top with the beef salad, and serve immediately.

Serves 8

■ Note

Thai or Vietnamese fish sauce is available in the ethnic section of many supermarkets, as well as in ethnic markets. If it is unavailable, substitute a splash or two of soy sauce.

chapter three
sandwiches & burgers

grilled quesadillas
with radish & tomato salsa

W ITH YOUR PORTABLE GRILL BY YOUR SIDE, anything's possible . . . even fresh, homemade quesadillas on the road. Before you head out, make the salsa; prepare the cilantro, scallions, and cheese and store them in resealable plastic bags. Whatever you do, don't overstuff the quesadillas: They should be fairly flat for easy flipping. And feel free to vary the ingredients: sliced roasted peppers (especially poblanos), sliced fresh or pickled jalapeños, guacamole, and shredded cooked chicken are all tantalizing possibilities.

RADISH & TOMATO SALSA

3 ripe medium tomatoes, seeded and chopped

½ cup trimmed and thinly sliced radishes

½ cup minced red or sweet white onion

1 jalapeño chile, seeded and minced

1 tablespoon minced fresh cilantro

¼ teaspoon salt

Ground red pepper, to taste

QUESADILLAS

Twelve 8-inch flour tortillas

3 cups grated (about 12 ounces)
   Monterey Jack cheese

6 tablespoons finely chopped fresh cilantro

6 slender scallions, finely chopped

1. Make the radish and tomato salsa: In a medium bowl, stir the tomatoes, radishes, onion, jalapeño, cilantro, salt, and ground red pepper together. Set aside and let stand for 30 minutes before serving.

2. Preheat the grill to medium.

3. Make the quesadillas: In batches, grill 6 tortillas on one side; turn and top each tortilla with ½ cup cheese, 1 tablespoon cilantro, and ⅙ of the chopped scallions, leaving a ½-inch border around the edge. Top each with another tortilla. Cook the quesadillas for 3 to 5 minutes on each side, until the cheese is melted and the tortillas are lightly browned.

4. Transfer the quesadillas to a cutting board and cut each into 4 or 6 wedges. Serve hot with radish and tomato salsa.

Serves 6

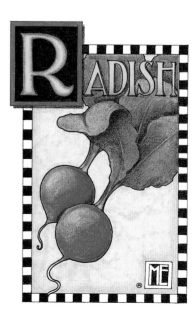

tomatillo burritos
with grilled corn

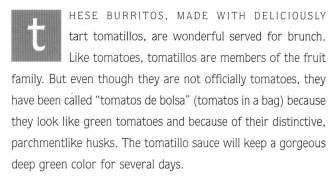

tHESE BURRITOS, MADE WITH DELICIOUSLY tart tomatillos, are wonderful served for brunch. Like tomatoes, tomatillos are members of the fruit family. But even though they are not officially tomatoes, they have been called "tomatos de bolsa" (tomatos in a bag) because they look like green tomatoes and because of their distinctive, parchmentlike husks. The tomatillo sauce will keep a gorgeous deep green color for several days.

6 ears fresh corn, husks and silks removed

10 fresh (about 1 pound) tomatillos, husked, rinsed, and quartered

1 white onion, finely chopped

½ cup finely chopped fresh cilantro

2 tablespoons vegetable oil

1 teaspoon sugar

1 garlic clove, minced

½ teaspoon salt

1 small fennel bulb, finely chopped

1 jalapeño chile, seeded and minced

Pinch of ground red pepper

3 tomatoes, seeded and chopped

Four 10-inch flour tortillas

¼ cup sour cream

1. Preheat the grill to medium-high and oil the rack. In a large pot, soak the ears of corn in cool water to cover for at least 10 minutes.

2. Grill the corn, turning frequently, for about 12 minutes, until the kernels have dark brown spots. Let the corn cool, then remove the kernels from the cobs.

3. In the bowl of a food processor, combine the tomatillos, ½ cup of the onion, the cilantro, 1 tablespoon of the oil, the sugar, garlic, and ¼ teaspoon of the salt. Process until the tomatillos are coarsely chopped.

4. In a large nonstick skillet, heat the remaining 1 tablespoon oil over medium-high heat. Add the remaining onion and the fennel. Saute, stirring, about 5 minutes, or until the fennel is softened. Stir in the corn, jalapeño, the remaining ¼ teaspoon salt, and pepper. Saute, stirring, until the mixture is heated through. Stir in 1 cup of the tomatillo mixture and the tomatoes and saute, stirring, until heated through.

5. Meanwhile, in a large dry skillet, warm each tortilla over medium heat for about 1 minute on each side. On a work surface, lay out the tortillas. Using about 1 cup of the corn mixture per tortilla, fill the center of each, fold in the sides and roll up. Arrange on serving plates.

6. Top each burrito with about ¼ cup of the remaining tomatillo sauce and 1 tablespoon of sour cream.

Serves 4

smoked turkey
with brie & arugula

eASY AND COOL, THIS SOPHISTICATED SANDWICH can be enjoyed on the back porch for Saturday lunch or for a light supper on a sultry evening. Peppery watercress stands in beautifully for arugula, if you prefer it. Whatever ingredients you ultimately use, choose only the freshest, and if you happen to have any homemade mayonnaise, by all means slather it on.

> About ½ cup mayonnaise
>
> Mustard, to taste
>
> 16 large slices light rye or or sourdough bread
>
> 1 large or 2 small bunches arugula,
>
> trimmed, rinsed, and spun dry
>
> 1 pound thinly sliced smoked turkey
>
> 3 to 4 ripe tomatoes, cut into
>
> ¼-inch-thick slices
>
> Salt and freshly ground pepper
>
> ¾ pound Brie, cut into long, thin slices

Spread the mayonnaise and mustard evenly on the bread. Place a few arugula leaves on each of 8 of the slices. Top each with a few slices of turkey and 2 tomato slices. Sprinkle with salt and a generous amount of pepper and place a few slices of Brie on each sandwich. Top with the remaining bread. Cut each sandwich in half on the diagonal and serve immediately.

Serves 8

tomatoes
& pesto sandwich

fLAVORFUL TOMATOES AND BASIL-SCENTED mayonnaise are a match made in heaven. Since this sandwich depends completely on the taste of the tomatoes, use only home-grown or heirloom varieties. If you can, use several different types of tomatoes—farmers' markets often offer them in a variety of colors, from yellow to red-and-green striped to almost purple. You could add lettuce to these sandwiches, but we like them with just the tomatoes in all their summery glory.

> ½ cup mayonnaise
>
> 3 tablespoons pesto, store-bought or homemade
>
> 16 large slices country or peasant-style bread,
>
> toasted
>
> 4 to 5 large ripe tomatoes, cut into
>
> ¼-inch-thick slices
>
> Freshly ground pepper, to taste

In a small bowl, combine the mayonnaise and pesto and mix well. Spread the mixture evenly on the toasted bread. Divide the tomato slices among 8 of the slices of bread, sprinkle generously with pepper, and top with the remaining bread. Cut each sandwich in half on the diagonal and serve immediately.

Serves 8

portobello
mushroom burgers

tHE ANNUAL FAMILY REUNION IS IN FULL SWING. Now comes the ancient rite of serving the burgers. But this year, it's something new—portobellos topped by a spirited spread, and there's no meat in sight.

6 tablespoons chicken broth or vegetable stock

2 tablespoons olive oil

2 teaspoons balsamic vinegar

1 teaspoon fresh thyme

¼ teaspoon salt, or to taste

¼ teaspoon freshly ground pepper, or to taste

4 medium portobello mushrooms (each about
    4 inches in diameter), stems removed

½ cup mayonnaise

2 tablespoons minced fresh chives, plus chive stems
    for garnish, if desired

1 garlic clove, mashed to a paste with a pinch of salt

1 teaspoon grated lemon zest

4 sandwich-size English muffins, split

8 small romaine leaves, rinsed and dried

8 slices ripe tomato

1. In a shallow baking dish just large enough to hold the mushrooms in a single layer, whisk together the chicken broth, oil, vinegar, thyme, and ⅛ teaspoon each salt and pepper. Add the mushrooms and marinate at room temperature, turning occasionally, for 30 minutes.

2. Preheat the grill to medium and lightly oil the rack.

3. Meanwhile, stir together the mayonnaise, chives, garlic mixture, lemon zest, and ⅛ teaspoon each salt and pepper in a small bowl. Cover and set aside.

4. Grill the mushrooms for about 4 minutes on each side, turning occasionally, until they are softened and cooked through. Grill the cut sides of the muffins, if desired.

5. Lightly spread the bottom muffin halves with the flavored mayonnaise. Top each with 2 romaine leaves on the bottoms, top with 1 mushroom, 2 tomato slices, a dollop of flavored mayonnaise (and a few chive stems, if using), and the muffin tops, and serve hot.

Serves 4

chutney turkey burgers
on sourdough

PICTURE A PICNIC TABLE TUCKED AWAY BY A stream and piled high with old-fashioned summer food: potato salad, coleslaw, watermelon, peach pie, and, of course, burgers. But these burgers aren't your typical variety: They have a sweet-and-hot taste, courtesy of the chutney. The fact that they're low-fat is an added fillip.

¾ cup mango chutney, large pieces finely chopped

1 tablespoon Dijon mustard

2 teaspoons fresh lime juice

1 pound ground turkey

¼ cup minced fresh parsley

2 scallions (white and tender green parts only), minced

½ teaspoon salt, or to taste

¼ teaspoon freshly ground pepper, or to taste

Eight ½-inch-thick slices sourdough bread

16 arugula sprigs

4 thin slices red onion

1. Preheat the grill to medium and lightly oil the rack.

2. In a small bowl, stir ½ cup of the chutney, the mustard, and lime juice together. Set aside.

3. In a medium bowl, gently but thoroughly combine the turkey, the remaining ¼ cup chutney, the parsley, scallions, salt, and pepper. Form the turkey mixture into 4 patties, each slightly less than ¾ inch thick.

4. Grill the patties, turning once, for 5 to 7 minutes on each side for medium-rare. Grill or toast the bread, if desired.

5. Spread 4 slices of the bread with the reserved chutney mixture. Top each with 4 arugula sprigs, 1 onion slice, and a turkey patty. Top with the remaining bread and serve hot.

Serves 4

Beyond Charcoal

It's time to forsake standard briquets and try something new. The next time you're grilling, consider these flavorful possibilities. Many gas grills have a special compartment designed to hold scented wood and herbs.

• For fish and shellfish, toss seaweed or kelp into the flame or sit them directly on the grill itself. Branches of lavender, thyme, rosemary, and sage suit meats, vegetables, and poultry. Fresh or dried, they'll need to be soaked for a half hour in water beforehand.

• Lightly crack unshelled almonds, pecans, or walnuts, soak them for a half hour, then toss them on the fire.

grilled hamburgers with
shiitake & red onion relish

WE ALWAYS WONDERED HOW WIMPY OF "POPEYE" fame could put away burger after burger without getting bored. This recipe could explain everything: Ordinary burgers become something special topped with a relish of fresh shiitake (or white button) mushrooms and red onion. You'd be wise to make the relish several hours ahead to give the flavors time to marry.

2 tablespoons olive oil

2 medium red onions, thinly sliced

½ pound large shiitake mushrooms, stems removed
    and discarded and caps thinly sliced

¼ cup chicken broth or water

1 tablespoon balsamic vinegar

1 tablespoon packed light brown sugar

¾ teaspoon fresh thyme

½ teaspoon salt, or to taste

¼ teaspoon freshly ground pepper, or to taste

1 pound ground beef

4 seeded rolls, split

1. Preheat the grill to medium.

2. In a medium nonstick skillet, heat the oil over medium-high heat. Add the onions and cook, stirring, for about 5 minutes, or until softened. Add the mushrooms, broth, vinegar, sugar, thyme, ¼ teaspoon salt, and ⅛ teaspoon pepper and cook, stirring, until the mushrooms are softened and most of the liquid has evaporated. Set aside at room temperature, covered, until ready to serve.

3. In a medium bowl, season the ground beef with the remaining ¼ teaspoon salt and ⅛ teaspoon pepper and gently but thoroughly combine. Form the beef into 4 patties, each about ¾ inch thick.

4. Grill the patties, turning once with tongs, for 5 to 7 minutes on each side for medium-rare. Grill the rolls, if desired.

5. Place a hamburger patty on the bottom half of each roll, top with the shiitake mushroom mixture, add the top halves of the rolls, and serve hot.

Serves 4

a company picnic

probably the single factor that keeps most of us from having enough picnics is the prospect of lugging lots of stuff to some idyllic, faraway spot—and then discovering that we've forgotten the salt and pepper. When you set up a picnic at home on the deck or patio, you don't have to worry. Instead, get creative.

SANDWICH-BUILDING PLANS

smoked chicken with mango chutney on seven-grain bread

shrimp, cucumber, and radishes with dill butter on pumpernickel

roasted red peppers, prosciutto, and mozzarella with balsamic vinegar on rustic italian bread

tapenade, sliced tomatoes, and watercress on a croissant

EXTRAS FOR THE BASKET

grill-sweetened bell peppers
(page 15)

picnic-style deviled eggs
(page 19)

Thermos of cold cucumber soup with yogurt & mint
(page 28)

coleslaw asian style
(page 32)

chocolate-chunk blondies in waxed paper bags
(page 122)

ON HAND FOR PICNIC STYLE

Andres Segovia guitar music on CD

mesh-wrapped citronella candles

buckets of zinnias and sunflowers

plaid stadium blankets

a dozen kerosene lanterns for nightfall

enamelware cups, bowls, and plates

Decorate the Deck

This is going to be your prettiest picnic ever. The key is to keep it casual—even a bit rustic—yet wonderfully stylish:

- Wrap sandwiches in waxed paper or brown kraft paper, tie with rickrack, and add stick-on labels with guests' names so the bundles can double as place cards.

- Set the table with vintage lunch boxes, plaid metal picnic hampers, and vintage Thermoses standing in for vases.

- Use bandanas or dish towels as napkins.

- A birthday-picnic centerpiece: Fill mason jars with marbles, then insert pinwheels.

santa fe burgers
with avocado relish

STRING UP THE CHILE-PEPPER LIGHTS AND SET the table with those cactus-shaped salt and pepper shakers. Start the menu with Farm-Fresh Creamy Corn Soup (page 27).

½ ripe Hass avocado, peeled and chopped

¼ cup sour cream

¼ cup "thick and chunky" salsa

1 tablespoon chopped fresh cilantro

1 teaspoon chili powder

½ teaspoon ground cumin

½ teaspoon ground coriander

¼ teaspoon salt

¼ teaspoon ground red pepper

1 pound ground beef

4 seeded rolls, split

8 thick slices ripe tomato

8 small romaine leaves

1 small red onion, sliced into rings (optional)

1. Preheat the grill to medium-high and oil the rack.

2. In a small bowl, stir together the avocado, sour cream, salsa, and cilantro. Set aside at room temperature.

3. In another small bowl, stir together the chili powder, cumin, coriander, salt, and pepper. In a medium bowl, sprinkle the beef with the spices and gently combine, handling the mixture as little as possible. Form 4 patties, each about ¾ inch thick.

4. Grill the patties for 5 to 7 minutes on each side for medium-rare; grill the rolls, cut side down, for about 2 minutes.

5. Spread the bottom half of each roll with the avocado mixture; top with a hamburger patty, 2 tomato slices, 2 lettuce leaves, and red onion, if using. Add the top halves of the rolls and serve, accompanied by the remaining avocado mixture.

Serves 4

creamy blue-cheese
hamburgers

dON'T LIMIT THESE BURGERS TO THE USUAL summer cookouts: Imagine how satisfying this richly flavored blue-cheese special would be after a day of leaf-raking or cross-country skiing, followed by an apple or gingerbread dessert. For the more virtuous among us, the blue-cheese topping also makes a terrific dip for vegetable crudités.

BLUE-CHEESE TOPPING

½ cup mayonnaise

2 ounces blue cheese, crumbled

1½ tablespoons finely chopped fresh chives

Generous pinch of freshly ground pepper

2 pounds ground beef

1½ teaspoons salt

¾ teaspoon freshly ground pepper, or more
　　to taste

1. Make the blue-cheese topping: In a small bowl, combine the mayonnaise and cheese and stir with a fork until well blended. Stir in the chives and pepper. Cover and refrigerate until ready to serve. The topping can be made up to 1 day ahead.

2. Preheat the grill to medium-high and oil the rack.

3. In a medium bowl, combine the ground beef, salt, and pepper. Shape the mixture into eight ¾-inch-thick patties.

4. Grill the hamburgers, turning once, until cooked through, 6 to 8 minutes per side. Spoon a generous dollop of blue-cheese topping on each burger and serve immediately.

Serves 8

Burger Bash

Semi-Veggie Burgers: Add chopped spinach and mashed chickpeas to ground beef.

Lamb-burgers: Add chopped parsley, chopped nuts, and grated onion to ground lamb; top lamb-burgers with melted Cheddar or Roquefort. Serve on toasted English muffins.

Mexiburgers: Combine ground beef with chile sauce and ground red pepper. Set up a burger bar with grilled onions, diced scallions, sliced tomatoes, lettuce, sliced avocado, grated Cheddar, sour cream, and, of course, salsa and pickled jalapeños.

Francoburgers: Combine about ¼ cup of a red Burgundy with 1½ pounds of ground beef and add a pinch or two of dried thyme. Serve on toasted slices of French bread and top with herb butter and sauteed mushrooms.

SANDWICHES
& BURGERS

the "new"
b.l.t. deluxe

GUESTS FOR THE WEEKEND? SATURDAY LUNCH doesn't require that you slave away in the kitchen. With the right ingredients and a couple of skillets, you're well on your way to a memorable backyard picnic feast. We've given the bacon-lettuce-and-tomato a makeover, stuffing it with arugula and applewood-smoked bacon. It comes on rustic sourdough bread, too. For even more flavor, make your own garlicky aïoli and use it instead of regular mayonnaise.

■ Variations

For more substantial sandwiches, add slices of smoked turkey or smoked chicken—in that case, you may prefer to use regular thick-sliced bacon rather than applewood-smoked. And try watercress with the turkey or chicken instead of arugula.

16 thick slices applewood-smoked bacon (about
   ¾ pound)
½ cup mayonnaise
16 large slices sourdough bread, toasted
2 bunches arugula
3 to 4 large ripe tomatoes, cut into
   ¼-inch-thick slices
Salt and freshly ground black pepper, to taste

1. In two large skillets, cook the bacon until it is crisp. Transfer to paper towels to drain.

2. Spread the mayonnaise evenly over the toasted bread. Place a few arugula leaves on each of 8 of the slices and top each with 3 tomato slices. Sprinkle the tomatoes with salt and pepper, place 2 slices of bacon on each, and top with the remaining slices of toast. Cut each sandwich in half on the diagonal and serve immediately.

Serves 8

pan bagnat
à la niçoise

SANDWICHES
& BURGERS

YOU'VE STAKED OUT A FRONT-ROW VIEW AT the Memorial Day parade. But even though lunchtime is far away, you're feeling famished already. Take your cue from the French and try this tasty mid-morning snack, a pan bagnat (which in French means bathed, wet, or soaked bread). Now you don't have to hear your tummy rumbling while you wait for the Jaycees to drive by in funny cars. Wrapped in foil, pan bagnat can be kept weighted overnight in the refrigerator—it's even better that way.

One 8-inch round loaf of bread, halved horizontally

1 garlic clove, halved

¼ cup olive oil

2 teaspoons red wine vinegar

Salt, to taste

Freshly ground pepper, to taste

3 ripe tomatoes, cut into thick slices

24 fresh basil leaves

One 6⅛-ounce can tuna packed in olive oil or water, drained

1 scallion (white and tender green part), finely chopped

2 teaspoons drained capers

12 Niçoise olives, pitted

1 hard-cooked egg, peeled and sliced

1. Remove some of the soft center of the bread to make a hollow. Rub each half with the cut side of the garlic clove, drizzle each half with about 1 tablespoon olive oil and 1 teaspoon vinegar, and season with salt and pepper.

2. Cover the bottom half of the bread with 1 sliced tomato, drizzle with olive oil, and top with 12 basil leaves.

3. In a small bowl, stir together the tuna, scallion, capers, and olives. Cover the basil with the tuna mixture. Add a layer of hard-cooked egg, then the remaining 2 tomatoes and the remaining 12 basil leaves. Drizzle with the remaining olive oil and 1 teaspoon vinegar; season with salt and pepper. Place the top of the bread on the sandwich and wrap tightly in foil.

4. Refrigerate the sandwich, weighted down, overnight. Let it stand for at least an hour before serving.

Serves 2

tomato, basil & tapenade
grilled-tuna sandwiches

tHESE SANDWICHES ARE SO SUBSTANTIAL that they could easily become dinner on a warm summer's eve. For the tapenade—a paste made of ripe olives, seasonings, capers, olive oil, and sometimes a bit of tuna—we've taken a shortcut with the prepared variety available in specialty food stores and many supermarkets. A little helpful hint: A hinged wire fish basket makes it infinitely easier to turn fish steaks and fillets on the grill.

1 tablespoon olive oil

1 tablespoon red wine vinegar

Salt, to taste

Freshly ground pepper, to taste

½ cup mayonnaise

3 tablespoons tapenade

Four ¾-inch-thick fresh tuna steaks (about 4 ounces each), rinsed and patted dry

4 seeded rolls, split

Romaine lettuce leaves, rinsed and spun dry

4 thick slices ripe tomato

8 large fresh basil leaves

1. Preheat the grill to medium-high.

2. In a small bowl, stir together the oil and vinegar and season with salt and pepper. In another small bowl, stir together the mayonnaise and tapenade; season with salt and pepper.

3. Brush the tuna with the oil mixture. Grill the fish, brushing with the oil mixture and turning once, for 6 to 8 minutes, until the fish is lightly browned on the outside but still red inside. If desired, grill the rolls, cut side down, for about 2 minutes.

4. Spread the interiors of the rolls with the mayonnaise mixture. Line each bottom half of roll with romaine leaves; top with tomato slices, basil leaves, and then the tuna. Add the top halves of the rolls and serve.

Serves 4

summer shack
lobster rolls

I N LOBSTER COUNTRY THEY SELL A ROLL that's made just for this sandwich. It looks like a hot dog bun, but is cut a little differently. If you don't live where lobsters are brought ashore, buy hot dog rolls, as we did. Often you can find brioche rolls at bakeries in the summertime—if you can, use them, for it's a heavenly combination. A tangy white Zinfandel or a sparkling Vouvray would dress up this hearty finger food nicely.

½ pound cooked lobster meat,
  picked over for shells

½ cup mayonnaise

1 teaspoon grated lemon zest

Salt, to taste

Freshly ground pepper, to taste

2 hot dog buns, toasted

1. In a small bowl, combine the lobster, mayonnaise, lemon zest, salt, and pepper.

2. Arrange the lobster mixture on the bottom of the hot dog buns. Finish the sandwich with a roll top.

Serves 2

▦ Note

Cook live whole lobsters for this recipe or take it easy and buy cooked lobster meat at your local fish market or supermarket. If you're not a purist, you might like to add slices of ripe tomatoes, fresh basil leaves, arugula, and/or romaine lettuce to this classic sandwich. Some have even been known to add celery, but we think they're best without.

spicy avocado & *shrimp fajitas*

a LLOW YOUR FAMILY AND GUESTS TO CUSTOMIZE their own fajitas. For a smorgasbord effect, offer additional options like black bean dip, minced chives, crumbled chèvre, and steamed broccoli florets.

2 scallions (white and tender green parts), trimmed
  and minced

3 tablespoons fresh lime juice

2 tablespoons vegetable oil

1 or 2 garlic cloves, mashed to a paste with
  ¼ teaspoon salt

½ teaspoon each ground cumin, coriander,
  and chili powder

¼ teaspoon ground red pepper, or to taste

1 pound medium shrimp, peeled and deveined

Eight 7- or 8-inch flour tortillas

1 cup prepared salsa, or Radish & Tomato Salsa
  (page 54)

1 ripe Hass avocado, peeled, seeded, and chopped

½ cup sour cream

1. Whisk together the scallions, lime juice, oil, garlic, cumin, coriander, chili powder, and red pepper in a medium bowl. Add the shrimp and marinate at room temperature, turning frequently, for 20 minutes.

2. Wrap the tortillas in foil and warm them in a hot oven.

3. Cook the shrimp, with the marinade, in a large skillet over medium heat, stirring constantly, for 3 to 4 minutes, just until the shrimp are cooked through and opaque. Be careful not to overcook.

4. Serve small platters of the shrimp, the warm tortillas wrapped in a cloth napkin, and bowls of salsa, avocado, and sour cream and have diners assemble their own fajitas.

Serves 4

chapter four

main courses

summer frittata
with squash & tomato

I F YOU'VE BEEN OUTDOORS AT THE ART FAIR all morning, you'll probably want to skip the grill and have something quick off the stove. This sunny, light frittata is just right for brunch or an early Sunday supper, perhaps dressed up with edible flowers like nasturtiums and calendula. Or serve it up as a sandwich on soft rolls. Frittatas are one of the most versatile dishes to serve outdoors. They can be flavored with virtually any ingredient—cheese, cooked meat or poultry, vegetables, even leftover pasta or rice—and you can reduce or expand the recipe to feed two or twenty.

2 tablespoons butter

2 red onions, thinly sliced

2 garlic cloves, minced

2 ripe medium tomatoes, seeded and chopped, plus
   wedges for garnish

1 small yellow summer squash, cut crosswise into thin
   rounds, then cut into thin strips

¼ cup finely shredded fresh basil

¼ teaspoon freshly ground pepper

8 large eggs

1 teaspoon salt

1. Preheat the oven to 350° F.

2. In a 10-inch nonstick ovenproof skillet, melt the butter over medium heat. Add the onions and garlic and cook, stirring occasionally, for about 10 minutes, or until the onions are light golden brown. Add the tomatoes, yellow squash, basil, and pepper. Cook for about 5 minutes, or until the squash begins to soften.

3. In a medium bowl, beat the eggs and salt together with a fork. Pour the egg mixture over the vegetables in the skillet and stir to blend. Cook over medium heat for about 3 minutes, or until the mixture just begins to set around the edge. Place the skillet in the oven for about 10 minutes, or until set.

4. Using a rubber spatula, loosen the frittata from the skillet and slide it onto a platter. Top with tomato wedges and serve.

Serves 4 to 6

rise and shine
breakfast bash

f or Mother's Day or Father's Day or a best friend's birthday, start on a celebratory note. Enjoy breakfast or a brunch party outdoors as the sun is climbing its way toward noon. Preparing the meal becomes performance art when it's done on the spot, with the toaster, maybe the waffle iron, and even the juicer set up right out on the terrace or deck.

BLEND-INS FOR BETTER BUTTER

minced fresh mint and dill

dried apricots plumped in boiling water, then finely chopped

minced bee balm and lovage

grated orange peel and minced lemon verbena

MORNING MUNCHING

pomegranate seeds and mint leaves sprinkled on ruby grapefruit halves

biscuits cut with daisy-shaped cutters

fresh fruit with orange-yogurt sauce

summer frittata with squash & tomato
(page 75)

Serving Up Sunshine

There's something about the sight of a coffee pot gleaming in the sunshine that reminds us of resort living. To create that aura of luxury at home, pile on the special touches outdoors:

- room-service amenities: toast in a proper silver rack and soft-boiled eggs nestled in vintage egg cups

- hot-pink table linens, sunny yellow plates, and an edible, tropical centerpiece of kiwi, mangoes, pineapple, and starfruit

- a spray of cymbidium orchids in a julep cup

- a color scheme of cool summer whites: ivory linens, mother-of-pearl-handled flatware, and a stack of hobnail milk-glass cake stands with tiers of berries and muffins

- "planted" teacups for each place setting (fill a cup with floral foam; cut the stems of several flowers short and at an angle, and insert; cover any visible foam with small flowers—spray roses or clover, for instance)

b.l.t.
pasta salad

a GREAT BUFFET DISH, THIS LIGHT ENTREE looks and tastes like summer. Cherry tomatoes are surprisingly easy to seed—just scoop out the seeds with a demitasse spoon.

8 ounces wagon-wheel or bow-tie pasta

2 tablespoons olive oil

2 tablespoons white wine vinegar

½ teaspoon salt

⅛ teaspoon freshly ground pepper

4 slices bacon, cut crosswise into ½-inch pieces

1 pint small red cherry tomatoes, halved and seeded

2 tablespoons finely chopped fresh parsley

2 tablespoons finely chopped fresh basil

1½ cups finely shredded romaine lettuce leaves

1. In a large pot of boiling salted water, cook the pasta according to package directions, or until al dente. Drain the pasta and transfer to a large bowl. Immediately stir in the olive oil, vinegar, salt, and pepper and let the mixture stand until it reaches room temperature. (The pasta salad can be prepared to this point up to a day ahead, covered, and refrigerated; bring to room temperature before proceeding.)

2. In a medium skillet, cook the bacon over medium heat, stirring, until crisp. Drain on paper towels and set aside.

3. Stir the bacon, cherry tomatoes, parsley, and basil into the pasta mixture. Taste and adjust seasonings, especially the salt.

4. To serve, line a large platter with the lettuce, and top with the pasta salad.

Serves 6

Kebab Construction Zone

Afraid you don't have the engineering expertise to put together beautiful, delicious, evenly cooked kebabs? Consider these basics:

- Mind the cooking times: Avoid mixing slow- and fast-cooking foods on the same skewer.

- Soak wooden skewers to prevent burning.

- Keep foods as close to their natural shapes as possible. Shrimp, starfruit, and cherry tomatoes are all naturals for kebabs.

- Use two skewers when grilling fragile food, to prevent it from falling into the fire.

- Serve savory kebabs—with vegetables, meat, or fish—intact, on a bed of hot rice or pasta. Serve sweet fruit kebabs with ice cream, sorbet, or pudding.

- Finish off kebabs with a cube of grilled bread (savory) or pound cake (sweet).

mushroom tortellini
with lemon cream & snap peas

tHIS EASY, DELICATE SAUCE IS DELICIOUS ATOP most kinds of pasta. We chose mushroom tortellini because of the way it so perfectly complements the lemon, snap peas, and herbs, but feel free to choose your favorite variety—chicken or cheese would both be wonderful in this recipe.

2 tablespoons unsalted butter

2 garlic cloves, minced

1 cup canned low-sodium chicken broth or vegetable broth

2½ teaspoons grated lemon zest

1 cup heavy cream

½ teaspoon salt, or to taste

⅛ teaspoon freshly ground pepper

½ pound sugar snap peas, cut on the diagonal into ½-inch pieces

1 tablespoon chopped fresh tarragon or 2 tablespoons chopped fresh flat-leaf parsley

1½ pounds mushroom tortellini

Freshly grated Parmesan cheese, for serving

1. In a large deep skillet, melt the butter over medium heat. Add the garlic and cook until softened, 1 to 2 minutes. Add the broth and lemon zest, increase the heat to medium-high, and bring to a simmer. Simmer, stirring occasionally, until the broth has reduced by half.

2. Add the cream, salt, and pepper, reduce the heat to medium, and bring to a simmer. Simmer gently, stirring occasionally, until the cream has reduced and thickened slightly, about 3 minutes. Add the snap peas and cook, stirring frequently, until the peas are bright green and crisp-tender, about 2 minutes. Stir in the tarragon and add salt if necessary.

3. Meanwhile, in a large pot of boiling salted water, cook the tortellini until just al dente, about 8 minutes (or follow instructions on the package).

4. Drain the tortellini and add to the sauce. Heat, stirring occasionally, until the pasta has absorbed some of the sauce, 2 to 3 minutes. Serve in shallow pasta bowls, with grated cheese on the side.

Serves 8

vegetable kebabs
with poblano quesadillas

tHESE VEGETARIAN KEBABS CROSS CULTURES from the Middle East to Mexico when you serve them with quesadillas. The dish is so festive looking that you'll want to make it often; it is easily customized to finicky palates by adding or deleting vegetables. It's healthful, too: Grilling is a terrific way to lock in vegetables' nutrients.

¼ cup vegetable oil

6 scallions (white and tender green parts), 2 finely chopped and 4 cut into 2½-inch lengths

3 thin slices lime

1 tablespoon fresh lime juice

1 teaspoon ground coriander

1 teaspoon ground cumin

1 bay leaf

2 garlic cloves, peeled and halved

½ teaspoon chili powder

¼ teaspoon salt

¼ teaspoon crushed red pepper flakes

1 small zucchini, cut into eight ½-inch rounds

1 small yellow squash, cut into eight ½-inch rounds

8 button mushrooms, trimmed

½ red bell pepper, cored, seeded, and cut into 1½-inch squares

½ yellow bell pepper, cored, seeded, and cut into 1½-inch squares

½ orange bell pepper, cored, seeded, and cut into 1½-inch squares

Eight 1½-inch pieces corn on the cob

4 whole jalapeño chiles

Eight 7-inch flour tortillas

1⅓ cups grated Monterey Jack cheese

1 poblano chile, roasted, peeled, seeded, and chopped

2 tablespoons finely chopped fresh cilantro

1. In a large bowl, stir together the oil, the 2 finely chopped scallions, the lime slices, lime juice, coriander, cumin, bay leaf, garlic, chili powder, salt, and pepper flakes. Let stand at room temperature for 10 minutes. Stir in the vegetables and marinate, stirring occasionally, for 1 hour at room temperature.

2. Soak thirteen 7-inch wooden skewers in water for 30 minutes. Preheat the grill to medium-high and oil the rack.

3. Thread the vegetables on skewers: two skewers each for the zucchini, the yellow squash, mushrooms, the 4 scallions cut into 2½-inch lengths, the mixed bell peppers, and the corn; and one skewer for the jalapeños.

4. Grill the vegetables, turning often, until tender: the mushrooms for about 8 minutes; the scallions, about 10 minutes; the corn, about 12 minutes; the squash, about 15 minutes; the peppers, 15 to 20 minutes; and the jalapeños, about 20 minutes.

5. Meanwhile, place 4 of the tortillas on a work surface. Evenly divide the grated cheese and the chopped poblano chile among the tortillas and top each with another tortilla. Just before serving, grill the quesadillas for about 2 minutes on each side, until the cheese is melted and the tortillas just begin to brown. Cut each quesadilla into halves or quarters, and arrange on serving plates.

6. Remove the vegetables from the skewers, divide them among the plates, and sprinkle them with the cilantro. Serve immediately.

Serves 4

MAIN COURSES

penne with
grilled ratatouille

tRADITIONALLY, RATATOUILLE, A DISH FROM the south of France, is made in a slow-simmering pot; this version is quicker but produces much the same dazzlingly succulent results.

1 each red and yellow bell pepper, cored,
   quartered, and seeded
Six ½-inch-thick eggplant slices
1 fennel bulb, trimmed and cut into
   1-inch-wide strips
1 medium zucchini, cut lengthwise into
   ¼-inch-thick slices
1 bunch scallions (white and tender green parts)
¼ cup olive oil
1 pound penne or other short, tubular pasta
4 ripe plum tomatoes, peeled, seeded, and chopped
½ cup freshly grated Parmesan cheese
¼ cup finely chopped fresh basil
¼ cup finely chopped fresh parsley
1 garlic clove, minced
¾ teaspoon salt
¼ teaspoon grated orange zest
¼ teaspoon freshly ground pepper

1. Preheat the grill to medium-high and oil the rack.

2. Grill the vegetables, basting with 2 tablespoons of the olive oil and turning as needed, until softened and slightly charred on the outside: the peppers for 15 to 20 minutes; the eggplant, 15 minutes; the fennel, 10 to 15 minutes; the zucchini, 8 minutes; and the scallions 5 to 7 minutes. Remove the vegetables from the grill and let cool slightly.

3. Meanwhile, in a large pot of boiling salted water, cook the pasta according to package directions, or until al dente. Drain in a colander, reserving ½ cup of the pasta cooking water.

4. While the pasta is cooking, cut the grilled vegetables into ½-inch pieces.

5. Combine the pasta, the grilled vegetables, the remaining 2 tablespoons olive oil, the plum tomatoes, Parmesan cheese, basil, parsley, garlic, salt, orange zest, pepper, and enough of the reserved cooking water to make a sauce. Stir until combined well. Serve hot or at room temperature.

Serves 8

chicken breasts with
plum salsa

MAIN COURSES

a WARM-WEATHER VERSION OF CHICKEN WITH stewed prunes (which, after all, are just dried plums), this entree lets you take advantage of the abundance of summer plums, from sparkling yellow Kelseys and sweet red Santa Rosas to small, intensely flavored Italian purples. This fruit salsa works beautifully with most any sort of grilled poultry, not to mention grilled pork tenderloin.

Bird Basics

Don't just settle for chicken: Birds of all feathers are suited to grilling and smoking, including rock Cornish game hen, quail, duck, squab, guinea hen, pheasant, and turkey.

Sear the pieces skin side down in a hot skillet. Then the parts can be cooked on a covered grill over indirect heat until the meat at the bone is opaque and juices from the joint run clear. Doneness test: Pierce the bird with a long-handled fork or a metal or bamboo skewer, or cut into the bird with a sharp knife and take a look at the flesh. For chicken, an instant-read thermometer should read 160°F for breast meat and 170°F for dark meat.

PLUM SALSA

4 ripe plums, pitted and chopped

¼ cup finely chopped red onion

¼ cup finely chopped yellow bell pepper

1 jalapeño chile, seeded and finely minced

1 tablespoon olive oil

2 teaspoons seasoned rice vinegar

2 tablespoons finely chopped fresh cilantro

½ teaspoon salt

¼ teaspoon freshly ground pepper

4 boneless, skinless chicken breast halves

1. Preheat the grill to medium-high and oil the rack.

2. Make the plum salsa: In a medium bowl, combine the plums, red onion, bell pepper, jalapeño, olive oil, vinegar, cilantro, ¼ teaspoon salt, and ⅛ teaspoon pepper. Set aside at room temperature.

3. Season the chicken with the remaining ¼ teaspoon salt and ⅛ teaspoon pepper.

4. Grill the chicken, turning once, for 10 to 12 minutes, until golden brown and just cooked through.

5. To serve, arrange the chicken on four plates and serve hot, topped with the plum salsa.

Serves 4

black bean salad
with grilled chicken

tHIS SOUTHWESTERN SALAD ENTREE IS BEST when it has been prepared a few hours in advance to let the flavors intensify. The texture and taste of the beans are a wonderful complement to the grilled chicken. Serve a fresh salsa alongside for even more color and zing.

1½ pounds boneless, skinless chicken breasts

Olive oil, for brushing

Salt and freshly ground pepper

4 ears corn, husked

Three 15½-ounce cans black beans, rinsed
    and drained

1 red bell pepper, cored, seeded, and cut
    into ¼-inch dice

½ red onion, finely chopped

2 jalapeño chiles, finely minced

3 tablespoons fresh lime juice

5 tablespoons vegetable oil

6 tablespoons finely chopped fresh cilantro

1. Preheat the grill to medium.

2. Brush the chicken on both sides with olive oil and season generously with salt and pepper. Grill, turning once, until golden brown and cooked through, 6 to 8 minutes per side, depending on thickness. Transfer to a plate and let cool.

3. Shred the chicken into bite-size pieces (or cut it into bite-size chunks). Cover and refrigerate while you make the salad.

4. With a sharp knife, cut the corn kernels from the cobs. In a large bowl, combine the corn, black beans, bell pepper, red onion, and jalapeños. Stir in the lime juice, then stir in the vegetable oil. Season with 1 teaspoon salt, or to taste.

5. Add the chicken and cilantro to the salad and toss to mix well. Cover and refrigerate, stirring once or twice, for 1 hour, or until ready to serve. (The salad can be made up to 8 hours in advance.)

6. Just before serving, taste the salad and add additional salt if needed.

Serves 8

pepper-spiced
fried chicken

SOMEHOW, FRIED CHICKEN JUST SEEMS RIGHT for July 4th, when a group of friends converges at the beach or town park for a pyrotechnics display and lots of great food. Of course, toting a bucket to a daytime picnic is just as wonderful. Because it's spicy, this version is not particularly for young kids, but is great chilled for adult picnics or right out of the skillet with warm potato salad—and strawberry shortcake for dessert.

½ cup buttermilk

½ lemon, thinly sliced

1 to 3 jalapeño chiles, seeded and minced

½ teaspoon ground red pepper

One 2½- to 3-pound fryer chicken, cut into
     10 pieces and trimmed, wing tips discarded

Vegetable oil for frying (at least 2 cups)

1 cup all-purpose flour

2 teaspoons salt

½ teaspoon freshly ground pepper

1. In a large bowl, stir the buttermilk, lemon slices, jalapeño, and red pepper together until combined well. With a fork, poke about 20 holes in each piece of chicken; place the chicken in the bowl. Marinate the chicken, covered and chilled, for 2 hours, turning occasionally. Remove the chicken from the refrigerator 30 minutes before frying and let stand at room temperature. Discard the lemon slices.

2. In a large skillet, heat the oil over medium-high heat to 375°F; the oil should be about ¾ inch deep.

3. While the oil is heating, stir together the flour, salt, and pepper on a plate. Roll each piece of chicken in the flour to coat thoroughly and shake off the excess. Transfer the chicken to a wire rack.

4. Fry the chicken, in two batches, for about 10 minutes on each side, until the chicken is cooked through. If the oil begins to smoke, reduce the heat; if the oil stops bubbling around the chicken pieces, increase the heat. Remove chicken from the pan with tongs and drain on paper towels. Serve hot, warm, room temperature, or chilled.

Serves 4

piquant mango &
chicken salad

W HAT A LOVELY DISH TO SERVE OUTDOORS. Fruit and chicken is a rewarding combination, sophisticated enough for a dinner party and sweet enough to please the children. If you can't get a mango, substitute 1½ cups chopped fresh pineapple. Other delicious options: whole strawberries, diced papaya, or sliced plums.

⅓ cup vegetable oil

1 teaspoon grated lemon zest

⅓ cup fresh lemon juice (about 2 lemons)

1 tablespoon brown sugar

½ teaspoon salt

¼ teaspoon crushed red pepper flakes

4 boneless, skinless chicken breasts

2 large bunches watercress, large stems discarded

1 small red onion, cut into rings

1 large ripe mango, peeled, seeded, and cut
    into ¾-inch pieces

1. Preheat the grill to medium-high and oil the rack.

2. In a small bowl, whisk together the oil, lemon zest and juice, brown sugar, salt, and pepper flakes. In a medium bowl, combine the chicken with ⅓ cup of the well-stirred lemon juice mixture and marinate, turning occasionally, at room temperature for 20 minutes.

3. In a large bowl, toss together the watercress and red onion; refrigerate, covered, until ready to serve.

4. Grill the chicken for 5 to 6 minutes on each side, until it is just cooked through. Transfer the chicken to a cutting board. When cool enough to handle, cut the chicken breasts diagonally into ½-inch-thick slices.

5. Add the mango and the remaining lemon juice mixture to the greens and toss well. Arrange the greens on four serving plates and top with the sliced chicken.

Serves 4

rosemary-lemon
butterflied chicken

OPENED LIKE A BOOK AND GENTLY FLATTENED, butterflied chicken takes far less time to grill than a whole chicken. Poultry shears do the best job of cutting the chicken, or have your butcher do it for you. Remember: Chicken can dry out quickly on the grill, so watch it carefully and do not overcook.

Two 3½- to 4-pound chickens

8 garlic cloves, smashed into pieces

¼ cup coarsely chopped fresh rosemary

¼ cup fresh lemon juice

2 tablespoons olive oil

Salt and freshly ground pepper

1. With kitchen shears, cut down along both sides of the backbone of each chicken and remove the backbone. Turn the chickens skin side up and press down hard on the breasts to flatten them slightly.

2. In a large baking dish or shallow bowl, combine the garlic, rosemary, lemon juice, and olive oil. Add the chicken, turning to coat with the marinade. Cover and refrigerate, turning occasionally, for 1 to 3 hours.

3. Preheat the grill to medium.

4. Remove the chicken from the marinade, letting the excess drain off, and season generously on both sides with salt and pepper. Discard the marinade. Place the chicken skin side down on the grill and cook for about 15 minutes, or until the skin is well browned. Turn the chicken and cook for 20 to 25 minutes longer, until the juices run clear when the thigh is pierced. (If the chicken begins to brown too much before it is cooked through, move it to a slightly cooler part of the grill.)

5. Cut the chicken into serving pieces and serve hot.

Serves 8

A Grilling Potager

Plan your garden to supply vegetables and herbs for the grill. Try these pairings:

basil: tomatoes, potatoes, eggplant, squash, chicken, beef, lamb

chives: corn, tomatoes, potatoes, chicken

cilantro: corn, lamb, fish, shellfish

mint: eggplant, lamb, tuna

oregano: squash, eggplant, beef, swordfish

rosemary: mushrooms, potatoes, chicken, beef, lamb

sage: potatoes, eggplant, chicken, lamb, fish

tarragon: potatoes, mushrooms, chicken, beef

red-wine & garlic
marinated skirt steak

SKIRT STEAK IS A VERY FLAVORFUL CUT OF beef—it's the traditional meat for fajitas. Flank steak makes a good substitute; it's thicker than skirt steak, though, so increase the grilling time slightly, as necessary. Whichever steak you use, be sure to slice it against the grain, on a diagonal, or the meat will be chewy.

RED-WINE & GARLIC MARINADE

1½ cups dry red wine

⅓ cup soy sauce

5 cloves garlic, minced

2½ to 3 pounds skirt steak

8 medium portobello mushrooms, stems removed and caps wiped clean

¼ cup olive oil

2 garlic cloves, minced (optional)

Salt and freshly ground pepper

1. Make the marinade: Combine the wine, soy sauce, and garlic in a large glass baking dish or other shallow container. Add the steak and turn to coat. Cover and refrigerate for at least 1 and up to 4 hours, turning the meat occasionally.

2. Prepare a medium-hot fire in a grill.

3. Put the mushrooms in a large shallow bowl. Drizzle the olive oil over them, carefully turning them once or twice. Sprinkle with the garlic, if using, and season with salt and pepper.

4. Set the mushrooms, gill side down, on the grill and cook for 4 to 6 minutes, until they start to release their juices. Turn the mushrooms and cook until tender and juicy, 4 to 6 minutes longer. Transfer to a cutting board and let cool slightly, then cut into thick slices. Place in a bowl and cover to keep warm.

5. Meanwhile, remove the steak from the marinade, discard the marinade, and season the steak with salt and pepper. Grill, turning once, until medium-rare to medium, 2 to 3 minutes per side. (If it is overcooked, this cut of steak will be tough.) Transfer the steak to a cutting board and cut across the grain, on a diagonal, into thin slices.

6. Arrange slices of steak on individual plates, top with the mushrooms, and serve.

Serves 8

grilled beef tenderloin
with california salsa

jUST BECAUSE WE CALL FOR A SUMMERY SALSA as an accompaniment, don't limit this dish to warm weather. Grilling is a four-season activity, and grilled tenderloin is the sine qua non of meals. In fall and winter, substitute an herb butter or pesto sauce for the salsa. If you're unsure about doneness, have an instant-read thermometer on hand and cook the beef to 130°F for medium-rare.

SUMMER SALSA

3 ears sweet corn, husks and silks removed

16 cherry tomatoes, quartered

1 ripe Hass avocado, peeled, pitted, and finely chopped

¼ cup finely chopped red onion

8 fresh basil leaves

6 tablespoons vegetable oil

4 teaspoons fresh lime juice, or to taste

1 garlic clove, minced

Salt and freshly ground pepper, to taste

One 4- to 5-pound beef tenderloin, trimmed

1. Preheat the grill to medium.

2. Make the summer salsa: Using a sharp knife, cut the corn kernels from the cobs and place in a bowl. Add the cherry tomatoes, avocado, red onion, 4 of the basil leaves, finely shredded, 3 tablespoons of the oil, the lime juice, and the garlic; season with salt and pepper.

3. On a platter, drizzle the beef with the remaining 3 tablespoons oil, season with salt and pepper, and turn to coat.

4. On an oiled rack set 2 to 3 inches above the heat source, sear the tenderloin, turning occasionally, for about 15 minutes, or until browned on all sides. Raise the grill rack or set the tenderloin on the side where the heat is less intense. Cook, turning occasionally, for about 20 minutes longer for medium-rare, or to desired doneness. Let the beef stand on a cutting board for 10 minutes.

5. To serve, thinly slice the tenderloin and transfer the slices to a platter. Cut the remaining 4 basil leaves into fine shreds and sprinkle atop the sliced beef. Serve the salsa on the side, in a small serving bowl.

Serves 8 to 10

scallion & tomato
sirloin kebabs

t HIS IS DEFINITELY FIESTA FOOD! DON'T LET the fact that this meal is easy to clean up—the salad and kebabs are on same plate—sway you. It's exceptionally delicious. You can vary the recipe endlessly: Substitute chicken for beef and use a dry white wine, white wine vinegar, and fresh rosemary in the marinade instead, or adapt it for vegetarian tastes by leaving out the meat and substituting cut-up vegetables of your choice. An even better idea: Let guests decide how they want to build their own kebabs.

5 tablespoons olive oil

2 tablespoons dry red wine

2 tablespoons chile sauce

2 tablespoons finely chopped fresh parsley

2 tablespoons red wine vinegar

2 teaspoons prepared horseradish

2 teaspoons fresh thyme

2 garlic cloves, peeled and halved

1 pound boneless top sirloin, cut into twenty
    1½-inch squares

Twelve 2½-inch pieces of scallion

Salt, to taste

Freshly ground pepper, to taste

12 tiny yellow plum tomatoes

8 red cherry tomatoes

8 cups mixed greens or shredded romaine lettuce

1. Preheat the grill to medium-high. Soak four 12-inch wooden skewers in water to cover for 30 minutes.

2. Meanwhile, in a large bowl, stir together 2 tablespoons of the oil, the wine, chile sauce, parsley, 1 tablespoon of vinegar, the horseradish, thyme, and garlic; let stand for 10 minutes. Stir in the beef and scallions and marinate, stirring occasionally, for 20 minutes at room temperature.

3. In a large bowl, whisk together the remaining 3 tablespoons oil and the remaining 1 tablespoon vinegar and season with salt and pepper. Set aside.

4. Thread the beef and vegetables onto the four skewers in the following order: beef, scallion, yellow tomato, beef, red tomato, beef, scallion, yellow tomato, beef, red tomato, scallion, beef, and yellow tomato.

5. Grill the beef and vegetables, turning often, for 12 to 14 minutes, until beef is medium-rare or cooked to desired doneness; season with salt and pepper halfway through cooking.

6. Add the greens to the oil and vinegar mixture, toss to coat, and transfer to four plates. Top each serving with a skewer and serve immediately.

Serves 4

grilled rib-eyes
with chimichurri sauce

CALLED "THE SAUCE OF LIFE" IN ARGENTINA, chimichurri makes a great marinade as well as a zesty serving sauce. Grilled and broiled meats, not to mention sandwiches, eggs, and broiled chicken, all take well to this simple garlic and herb sauce. So it's a good idea to make a little extra and refrigerate it—you'll use it often.

CHIMICHURRI SAUCE

1 large garlic clove, minced

½ teaspoon salt

1½ cups loosely packed fresh flat-leaf parsley leaves, minced

1 cup loosely packed fresh cilantro leaves, minced, plus additional for garnish

¾ cup olive oil

2 tablespoons red wine vinegar

½ teaspoon crushed red pepper flakes

Two 2-inch-thick boneless rib-eye steaks (about 2½ pounds total), trimmed

Salt and freshly ground pepper, to taste

1. Preheat the grill to medium-high and oil the rack.

2. Make the chimichurri sauce: On a cutting board, with the side of a chef's knife, mash the garlic with the salt to a smooth paste. In a medium bowl, stir the garlic mixture with the parsley, cilantro, olive oil, vinegar, and crushed red pepper until combined well.

3. Pat the steaks dry and season with salt and pepper. Grill, covered, turning the steaks once, for 12 to 15 minutes for medium-rare, or to desired doneness.

4. Transfer the steaks to a cutting board and let stand for 10 minutes. With a sharp knife, cut the steaks across the grain and at a slight angle into thin slices. Arrange the slices on heated plates, sprinkle with cilantro, and serve with the sauce.

Serves 4 to 6

rosemary & garlic
lamb chops

OR A SPECIAL OCCASION OR "JUST BECAUSE," this grilled dish makes an elegant statement without requiring that you have a degree from culinary school. We'll admit that the classic rosemary-garlic marinade combo is nothing new—but why tamper with a classic?

MAIN COURSES

16 loin or rib lamb chops

2 tablespoons fresh rosemary

4 large garlic cloves, slivered

3 tablespoons olive oil

Salt and freshly ground pepper

1. Put the lamb chops in a large shallow bowl or large baking dish, scatter the rosemary and garlic over them, and drizzle with the olive oil, turning to coat. Cover and marinate in the refrigerator for 30 minutes to 2 hours, turning occasionally.

2. Preheat the grill to medium-high.

3. Remove the lamb chops from the marinade, scraping off any slivers of garlic, and season generously on both sides with salt and pepper. Grill, turning once, for 8 to 12 minutes, depending on the thickness, for medium-rare; do not overcook. Serve immediately.

Serves 8

Secret Sauces

We all have our favorite marinades—and sometimes, even the most dedicated cook resorts to opening one of those magic bottles of premade sauce. Those sauces can be good, but it only takes a few minutes to create your own fresh-tasting marinade that does justice to a fine cut of lamb or beef or a just-picked vegetable. Try these pairings:

beef: olive oil, green peppercorns, minced onion, and minced fresh marjoram

green vegetables: rice vinegar, minced fresh dill, and bay leaf

orange and yellow vegetables: orange juice, cinnamon, nutmeg, and fresh thyme

fish and lamb: lemon juice, olive oil, and salt and pepper

chicken: vegetable oil, dry white wine, garlic, onion, celery salt, fresh tarragon, and salt and pepper

venison: dry red wine, bay leaf, sliced onion, cloves, and fresh rosemary

grilled lamb chops
with cilantro pesto

gRILLED RIB OR LOIN LAMB CHOPS ARE SO tasty on their own they need little adornment. Here a fresh cilantro pesto sauce—made without cheese—provides just the right counterpoint; a small dollop on each chop is all you need. The pesto uses both the leaves and the tender stems, which are fragrant and flavorful (many Asian cuisines, in fact, use the cilantro roots as well in cooking). Two lamb chops per person make a generous serving; depending on the crowd you're expecting, you may want to cook only 12, rather than 16. The pesto would also be good on grilled tuna and other meaty fish.

CILANTRO PESTO

2 garlic cloves, smashed

1 cup packed fresh cilantro

2½ tablespoons olive oil

1 tablespoon unsalted butter, at room temperature

Generous pinch of salt

Freshly ground black pepper to taste

16 loin or rib lamb chops

Salt and freshly ground pepper

1. Make the cilantro pesto: With the food processor running, add the garlic and process until finely minced. Add the cilantro, oil, butter, salt, and pepper and process to a puree. Cover and refrigerate until ready to use. The pesto can be made up to 1 day ahead.

2. Preheat the grill to medium-high.

3. Season the lamb chops generously with salt and pepper. Grill, turning once, for 8 to 12 minutes, depending on the thickness, for medium-rare; do not overcook. Arrange on plates, top each chop with a small dollop of pesto, and serve immediately.

Serves 8

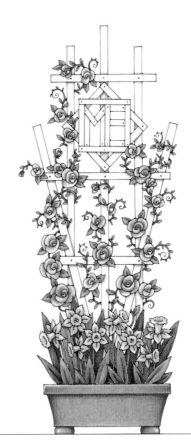

tandoori-marinated butterflied
leg of lamb

tHIS IS THE NIGHT TO PULL OUT ALL THE stops: a poolside party complete with tiki torches. Leg of lamb, boned and butterflied, is the perfect choice for a crowd. Its uneven thickness makes it possible to offer something for everyone—from medium-rare to well-done—all in one cut of meat. The marinade tenderizes the meat and fills the air with exotic scents. Serve with Warm Grilled Salad of Red Onion & Tomato (page 36), French Lentil Salad (page 48), and a full-bodied Zinfandel or Petite Sirah.

TANDOORI MARINADE

1½ cups plain low-fat yogurt

2 large garlic cloves, finely chopped

1 tablespoon finely chopped peeled ginger

1½ tablespoons paprika

1 teaspoon ground cumin

½ teaspoon ground cardamom (optional)

½ teaspoon ground red pepper

One 4- to 5-pound boneless leg of lamb, butterflied (have the butcher do this)

Coarse or kosher salt

1. Make the tandoori marinade: Combine the yogurt, garlic, ginger, and spices in a small bowl and mix well. (The marinade can be made up to 1 day ahead, covered, and refrigerated.)

2. Lay the lamb out flat on a cutting board and pound it gently with a meat mallet or the side of a heavy cleaver to even its thickness. Transfer the lamb to a large shallow baking dish and add the marinade, rubbing it all over the lamb to coat generously. Cover and refrigerate for 1 to 3 hours. (Do not marinate the lamb for longer than 3 hours, as the acidic yogurt may affect the texture of the meat.)

3. Preheat the grill to medium-high.

4. Sprinkle the lamb generously with coarse salt. Grill, turning once, 12 to 15 minutes per side, until the meat is cooked medium-rare to medium and the outside is beginning to char in spots. Transfer the lamb to a cutting board, cover loosely, and let rest for about 5 minutes.

5. Cut the lamb across the grain into slices and serve hot.

Serves 8

sage-scented
pork kebabs

hERE IS PROOF POSITIVE THAT GRILLED FARE should not be restricted to summer: This warming combination of sage and pork is just right on a winter's day. Just keep your mittens away from the flames!

½ cup minced shallots

¼ cup olive oil

2 tablespoons chicken broth

1 tablespoon balsamic vinegar

1 tablespoon plus ¾ teaspoon finely chopped
  fresh sage

2 garlic cloves, peeled and halved

1 pound lean pork butt, cut into twenty 1- to
  1½-inch cubes

3 tablespoons unsalted butter, at room temperature

Salt

Freshly ground pepper

Twenty ½-inch-thick round slices of zucchini
  (2 small)

Twelve ½-inch-thick slices French or Italian bread

1. Preheat the grill to medium-high and oil the rack. Soak four 12-inch wooden skewers in water to cover for 30 minutes.

2. In a large bowl, stir together the shallots, oil, chicken broth, vinegar, 1 tablespoon of the sage, and the garlic until combined well. Let stand for 10 minutes. Add the pork and marinate, stirring occasionally, for 20 minutes at room temperature.

3. Meanwhile, in a small bowl, stir together the butter, the remaining ¾ teaspoon sage, and a pinch each of salt and pepper. Set aside at room temperature.

4. Beginning and ending with zucchini, alternate the pork and zucchini slices on the skewers, using 5 pieces of each on each skewer; leave 1½ inches or more at the point of each skewer.

5. Grill the kebabs for 16 to 18 minutes, turning often, until the pork is just cooked through; season with salt and pepper halfway through cooking. During the last 4 or 5 minutes, grill the bread for 2 minutes per side, until golden brown. Spread one side of each slice of bread with the sage butter. Just before serving, thread 3 pieces of bread on the point of each skewer.

Serves 4

pork tenderloin
with peach jalapeño relish

aS SOUTHERN AS GRITS, GRILLED PORK TENDER-loin is a treat people don't enjoy often enough. The most sought-after cut of pork, the tenderloin is ideal for grilling because of its small size and melting texture. The spicy Caribbean-inspired relish makes generous leftovers that pair easily with chicken or fish. When you're in a hurry, pop open a jar of pineapple salsa or mango chutney instead.

PEACH JALAPEÑO RELISH

3 ripe peaches, peeled (see Note), pitted, and
  cut into ¼-inch dice

½ small red onion, halved lengthwise and very thinly
  sliced crosswise

1 to 2 jalapeño chiles, finely minced

3 tablespoons orange juice, preferably freshly
  squeezed

1½ tablespoons fresh lime juice

1½ tablespoons vegetable oil

½ cup slivered fresh cilantro

Salt and freshly ground pepper

2½ to 3 pounds pork tenderloin
  (2 or 3 tenderloins)

Vegetable oil, for brushing

Salt and freshly ground pepper

1. Make the peach jalapeño relish: In a medium bowl, combine the peaches, onion, and jalapeños. Stir in the orange juice, lime juice, and oil. Stir in the cilantro and season to taste with salt and pepper. The relish can be made up to 2 days ahead, covered, and refrigerated; serve chilled or at room temperature.

2. Preheat the grill to medium-high.

3. Lightly brush the pork with oil and sprinkle on all sides with salt and pepper. Grill, turning two or three times, for about 10 minutes, until well browned on all sides. Continue to cook, turning occasionally, for 12 to 15 minutes longer for medium. The pork should still be just pink in the center; an instant-read thermometer inserted in the thicker part of the meat will register 150°F. If the pork starts to brown too much before it's cooked, move it to a cooler part of the grill. Transfer to a cutting board and let rest, loosely covered with foil, for 5 to 10 minutes.

4. Cut the pork on the diagonal into slices about ½ inch thick. Serve immediately, with the relish.

Serves 8

■ Note

To peel peaches, immerse them in a pot of boiling water for 30 seconds to 1 minute (depending on ripeness), then peel off the skin with your fingers and/or a paring knife.

grilled pork chops
on arugula salad

t HE NEXT TIME YOU PRUNE YOUR FRUIT trees, save the wood for grilling, especially for pork chops, which take to fruitwood smoke like bread to butter. When buying pork chops for the grill, be sure they're at least ¾ inch thick, so they don't dry out.

8 cups arugula

2 plum tomatoes, halved lengthwise and thinly sliced

½ cup thinly sliced red onions

3 tablespoons olive oil

1 tablespoon balsamic vinegar

1 tablespoon minced fresh parsley

1 teaspoon Dijon mustard

½ teaspoon salt

¼ teaspoon crushed red pepper flakes

Four ¾-inch-thick boneless loin pork chops,
    3 to 4 ounces each

Pinch of freshly ground pepper

1. Preheat the grill to medium-high and oil the rack.

2. Place the arugula in a large bowl. In a small bowl, toss together the tomatoes and red onions. In a medium bowl, whisk together the oil, vinegar, parsley, mustard, ¼ teaspoon salt, and the red pepper flakes.

3. Season the pork chops with the remaining ¼ teaspoon salt and the freshly ground pepper. Grill the pork chops, turning once, 8 to 10 minutes, until just cooked through.

4. Meanwhile, pour one quarter of the vinaigrette into the tomato mixture and stir to combine. Toss together the arugula and half of the tomato mixture with the remaining vinaigrette; arrange on 4 serving plates. Top with the pork chops and the remaining tomato mixture.

Serves 4

tuna steaks
with salsa verde

SALSA VERDE MAY SOUND MEXICAN, BUT IT'S actually an Italian green herb and caper sauce. It's traditionally made with parsley, but you can add some fresh basil leaves to the mix. Anchovy lovers may want to add a teaspoon or so of anchovy paste or several whole anchovies. Salsa verde is also delicious on other meaty fish as well as on grilled chicken.

SALSA VERDE

1 garlic clove, cut into 2 or 3 pieces

1 cup packed fresh parsley leaves (or ¾ cup packed parsley and ¼ cup packed fresh basil)

3 tablespoons capers, drained

2 tablespoons fresh lemon juice

1 teaspoon Dijon mustard

½ cup olive oil

Salt and freshly ground pepper

Eight 5- to 6-ounce tuna steaks

Olive oil, for brushing

Coarse salt and freshly ground pepper

1. Make the salsa verde: With the machine running, drop the garlic through the feed tube of a food processor and process until finely minced. Add the parsley, capers, lemon juice, and mustard and process to a coarse paste. With the machine running, add the olive oil through the feed tube and process to a coarse puree. Season to taste with salt and pepper. (The sauce can be made up to 8 hours in advance, covered, and refrigerated; bring to room temperature before serving.)

2. Preheat the grill to medium-high.

3. Brush the tuna lightly on both sides with the olive oil and season generously with coarse salt and pepper. Grill, turning once, for 4 to 5 minutes per side for medium-rare, or to the desired doneness. Serve immediately, with a dollop of sauce on top of each tuna steak.

Serves 8

salade niçoise
with grilled tuna

MAIN COURSES

tHIS VERSION OF THE CLASSIC SALAD IS SO superior to the canned-tuna variety, you'll never go back. How very French of you to think of serving it.

1 pound small red-skinned potatoes, quartered lengthwise

½ pound haricots verts (thin French green beans) or green beans

VINAIGRETTE

2½ tablespoons fresh lemon juice

2 garlic cloves, smashed

¾ teaspoon Dijon mustard

½ cup olive oil

½ teaspoon salt, or to taste

¼ teaspoon freshly ground pepper

Eight 5- to 6-ounce tuna steaks

Olive oil, for brushing

Coarse salt and freshly ground pepper

2 heads butter lettuce

8 small tomatoes, quartered

4 hard-boiled eggs, quartered (optional)

½ cup thinly slivered fresh basil

4 ounces (about ⅔ cup) Niçoise olives

1. Put the potatoes in a large saucepan, add salted water to cover, and bring to a boil. Cook just until tender, about 15 minutes; drain and let cool. Meanwhile, bring another large saucepan of salted water to a boil. Add the beans and cook just until crisp-tender, 6 to 8 minutes. Drain and let cool. The potatoes and beans can be cooked early in the day; refrigerate separately, covered, until shortly before serving.

2. Make the vinaigrette: Combine the lemon juice, garlic, mustard, oil, salt, and pepper in a small jar, cover tightly, and shake to blend well. Set aside. The dressing can be made early in the day and refrigerated; bring to room temperature before using.

3. Preheat the grill to medium-high.

4. In a medium bowl, combine the potatoes with a generous 2 tablespoons of the dressing, tossing to coat. In another medium bowl, combine the beans with about 1½ tablespoons of the dressing, tossing to coat.

5. Brush the tuna on both sides with oil and season generously with coarse salt and pepper. Grill, turning once, for 4 to 5 minutes per side for medium-rare, or to the desired doneness.

6. Line individual serving plates with lettuce leaves. On one side of each plate, arrange a mound of beans, 4 tomato quarters, some potatoes, and 2 hard-boiled egg quarters, if using. Scatter the basil over the salads, and drizzle with the remaining vinaigrette (about 1 scant tablespoon each).

7. Slice each tuna steak and transfer to the plates. Scatter the olives over the salad and serve immediately.

Serves 8

grilled salmon
with pink grapefruit salsa

f OR AN ELEGANT ANNIVERSARY DINNER UNDER the trees, think pink. The pastel salsa and the salmon are a still life. If you prefer, use individual fillets rather than one large fillet. Salmon is heaven on the grill. The mild oiliness of the fish keeps it moist during cooking.

3 large pink grapefruit

6 radishes, trimmed and thinly sliced

⅓ cup finely chopped red onion

½ teaspoon salt

About ¼ teaspoon crushed red pepper flakes

One 2-pound salmon fillet (about
   1 inch at the thickest part), with skin on

2 tablespoons vegetable oil

2 tablespoons chopped fresh cilantro plus additional
   sprigs, for garnish

1. Preheat the grill to medium-high and oil the rack.

2. With a sharp knife, peel the grapefruit, removing all of the white pith. Over a medium bowl, remove the grapefruit sections by cutting along the membranes, letting the sections and juice fall into the bowl. Stir in the radishes, red onion, ¼ teaspoon salt, and a pinch of the red pepper flakes.

3. Brush the salmon with the oil and season with the remaining ¼ teaspoon salt and a pinch of red pepper flakes. Grill the salmon skin side up for 5 to 6 minutes, until a golden brown crust is formed; do not move the salmon fillet before the crust

is formed, or it may stick to the rack. With 2 pancake turners, turn the salmon carefully and grill the second side for 3 or 4 minutes, until just cooked through.

4. In a strainer, drain the grapefruit mixture. Transfer to a bowl, add the cilantro, and stir.

5. To serve, place the salmon skin side down on a large platter, top with the grapefruit mixture, and garnish with the cilantro sprigs, or divide among individual serving plates.

Serves 6

charmoula
grilled salmon

C HARMOULA IS A ZESTY MOROCCAN SAUCE that is delicious on many types of fish, including other meaty varieties like swordfish. It is also popular as a marinade for chicken and other types of poultry. Paprika, ground red pepper, and cumin give charmoula spicy heat, which is tempered by the lemon juice and a generous amount of cilantro. Couscous is a fine match to the salmon.

CHARMOULA

1½ tablespoons paprika

1 teaspoon ground red pepper

½ teaspoon ground cumin

3 garlic cloves, coarsely chopped

¼ cup fresh lemon juice

6 tablespoons olive oil

½ cup chopped fresh cilantro

Eight 5- to 6-ounce skinless salmon fillets

Coarse or kosher salt

Cilantro sprigs, for garnish

1. Make the charmoula: Combine all the ingredients in a blender and process until smooth, scraping down the sides of the container as necessary. (The charmoula can be made up to 2 days ahead, covered, and refrigerated.)

2. Put the salmon in a shallow baking dish and pour the charmoula evenly over the fillets, turning to coat. Cover and chill for 30 minutes to 1 hour, turning the salmon once or twice.

3. Preheat the grill to high and oil the grill rack.

4. Sprinkle the salmon with coarse salt. Place the fillets skinned side up on the grill, and grill, turning once, until just opaque throughout, 8 to 10 minutes. Serve immediately, garnished with cilantro sprigs.

Serves 8

let the games begin
day-into-dusk gathering

a supremely casual party gets everyone involved: kids dash through sprinklers, adults spread blankets on the grass and shuck corn, everyone scores at badminton. The moon clears the trees, and the party continues by lantern-light.

CONJURE
A CAMPFIRE
COOKOUT

a pair of bellows to fan
the fire

warm mulled cider ladled
from a cast-iron kettle

open-fire roasting
pans and an old-fashioned
popcorn popper

long twigs
and marshmallows—
and, for s'mores,
graham crackers and
chocolate squares

campfire songs and
ghost stories

a telescope and
stargazer's map of the
night sky

a children's tent
with toys, flashlights,
and sleeping bags

Party Survival Kit

Low stress is the name of the game. An unstructured, laid-back party can seem to run itself—if, that is, it's cleverly stocked with the right ingredients:

- A badminton net or croquet set can be the life of the party.

- Frisbees, soccer balls, hula hoops, water guns, and other inexpensive outdoor games are fun for everyone.

- If there will be wet swimsuits, be ready with a tree-to-tree clothesline.

- Butterfly nets: They're perfect as favors or as a "catch and release" pastime during a long, lazy afternoon.

- Fill a trunk with shawls, sweaters, and stadium blankets for cooler nights. Some guests will appreciate mosquito repellent.

- Kids who like to chase fireflies always need little wire cricket cages or jars with holes punched in the lids.

vegetable vinaigrette &
grilled halibut

I DECIDED TO THROW A PARTY, SOMETHING nice, something with an orchestra, by the sea with food, the tradewinds in the sea grapes," writes Thomas McGuane in his novel *Panama*. Here's the dish we imagine being served: Mild, sweet halibut glistening with a summer vegetable vinaigrette.

VEGETABLE VINAIGRETTE

½ zucchini, cut into ¼-inch dice

½ yellow squash, cut into ¼-inch dice

¼ pound green beans, cut into
　　¼-inch-long pieces

2 tablespoons fresh lemon juice

⅛ teaspoon Dijon mustard

6 tablespoons olive oil

½ teaspoon salt

Freshly ground pepper

2 small tomatoes, halved, seeded, and cut
　　into ¼-inch dice

Eight 6- to 8-ounce halibut steaks

Olive oil, for brushing

Salt and freshly ground pepper

1. Make the vinaigrette: Bring a medium saucepan of salted water to a boil. Add the zucchini and yellow squash and cook until just crisp-tender, 2 to 3 minutes. Immediately remove with a strainer and set aside to cool. Add the beans to the boil-ing water and cook until just crisp-tender, about 5 minutes. Drain and set aside to cool.

2. Preheat the grill to medium-high.

3. Meanwhile, in a medium bowl, combine the lemon juice and mustard, whisking to blend. Whisking constantly, drizzle the olive oil in a slow, steady stream. Add the salt and pepper to taste, then the zucchini, yellow squash, beans, and tomatoes, stirring gently to blend. Set aside at room temperature.

4. Brush the halibut on both sides with olive oil and season with salt and pepper to taste. Grill, turning once, until just cooked through, 8 to 12 minutes, depending on the thickness of the fish.

5. Place a fish steak on each dinner plate, spoon the vinaigrette over and around the fish, and serve immediately.

Serves 8

■ Note

If you cannot find halibut, substitute another meaty white-fleshed fish such as mako or swordfish. Sea bass and red snapper fillets are also delicious, but fillets are more delicate than steaks and have a tendency to stick to the grill, so use a grill basket or generously oil both the grill and the fish. Fillets will probably take slightly less time to cook.

cannellini bean salad
with grilled shrimp

C OMBINE CANNELLINI BEANS WITH SHRIMP for a dish that could be served at a Florence cafe. Serve this with crusty bread and a few slices of home-grown tomatoes. Look in a specialty store for imported cannellini beans, which tend to be smaller and more flavorful than the supermarket variety. But don't hesitate to substitute any white bean—or even black beans—for the cannellinis.

Three 15½-ounce cans cannellini beans,
   rinsed and drained
1 red onion, finely chopped
6 tablespoons olive oil
2 tablespoons balsamic vinegar
Salt and freshly ground pepper
⅔ cup finely chopped fresh flat-leaf parsley
2 pounds medium shrimp, peeled and deveined

1. In a large bowl, combine the beans, red onion, 3 tablespoons of the oil, the vinegar, 1 teaspoon salt, and ¼ teaspoon pepper. Add the parsley and toss to combine. The salad can be made early in the day, covered, and refrigerated; bring to room temperature before combining with the shrimp.

2. Preheat the grill to medium-high. If using wooden skewers, soak them in warm water for 15 minutes.

3. In a large bowl, toss the shrimp with the remaining 3 tablespoons olive oil, then season generously with salt and pepper, and toss again. Thread 5 shrimp (crosswise) onto each skewer.

4. Grill the shrimp, turning once, until opaque throughout, 3 to 5 minutes on each side. Slide the shrimp off the skewers into the bean salad, toss well, and serve.

Serves 8

Flowerless Bouquets

Good table decorations require little more than a hunt through your cupboards and a trip to the supermarket. You'll want to enjoy spring and summer flowers, but there is much more:

- A stack of vintage plates with interesting edges like scallops or gold rims, topped by a single perfect fruit.

- Silver cups or vases filled with bunches of silvery-green fresh sage or other herbs.

- Glossy purple eggplants and long curls of lemon zest piled in a shallow basket.

- Clear glass containers filled with cranberries to anchor cattails or other natural materials.

pasta with shrimp
& spicy cilantro sauce

tHINK OF THIS RECIPE AS THE FRAMEWORK for an infinite variety of snazzy meals. It could be made with chicken instead of shrimp. Or hold the shrimp and serve as a first course. Not in the mood for pasta? Try the zesty sauce as a topping for steaks or meaty fish.

SPICY CILANTRO SAUCE

4 cups packed coarsely chopped fresh cilantro (about 2 large bunches)

3 to 4 jalapeño chiles, coarsely chopped

4 garlic cloves, coarsely chopped

2 tablespoons minced peeled ginger

2 teaspoons salt, or more to taste

½ cup vegetable oil

¼ cup fresh lime juice

6 tablespoons olive oil

2 pounds medium shrimp, peeled and deveined

1½ pounds fine or regular linguine

1. Preheat the grill to medium-high. If using wooden skewers, soak them in warm water for 15 minutes.

2. Meanwhile, make the spicy cilantro sauce: In the bowl of a food processor, combine the cilantro, jalapeños, garlic, ginger, salt, vegetable oil, and 2 tablespoons of the lime juice and process to a coarse paste, scraping down the sides of the bowl as necessary. Transfer 3 tablespoons of the paste to a large shallow bowl. Add the remaining 2 tablespoons lime juice and the olive oil to the processor and process until well blended. Set this sauce aside. The sauce can be prepared several hours ahead; refrigerate the cilantro paste and sauce separately.

3. Add the shrimp to the reserved cilantro paste and toss to coat. Thread 5 shrimp crosswise onto each skewer.

4. In a large pot of boiling salted water, cook the linguine until it is al dente.

5. Meanwhile, grill the shrimp, turning once, until opaque throughout, 1 to 2 minutes on each side.

6. Drain the pasta and return it to the pot. Add the sauce and toss well. Slide the shrimp off the skewers, add to the pasta, and toss well. Serve immediately.

Serves 8

shrimp
in five spices

WHEN SUNSET IS IN HALF AN HOUR, MAKE this dish: It takes twenty minutes to marinate the shrimp and just ten minutes to cook on the stove.

2 tablespoons chicken broth

2 scallions, finely chopped

2 teaspoons Asian (toasted) sesame oil

1½ teaspoons minced peeled ginger

1½ teaspoons rice vinegar

1 teaspoon soy sauce

½ teaspoon Chinese five-spice powder

1 pound large shrimp, peeled and deveined

3 tablespoons vegetable oil

2 small red onions, halved and thinly sliced

Hot steamed white rice

1. In a medium bowl, whisk together the chicken broth, half the scallions, the sesame oil, ginger, vinegar, soy sauce, and five-spice powder. Add the shrimp and marinate, stirring frequently, for 20 minutes at room temperature.

2. In a wok or large skillet, heat the oil over medium-high heat and stir-fry the red onions until they begin to brown, about 3 minutes. Add the shrimp and marinade; stir-fry just until shrimp is cooked through, about 3 minutes; do not overcook. Arrange the shrimp on plates with the steamed white rice and serve sprinkled with the remaining scallions.

Serves 4

molasses-glazed
shrimp

tHIS PLEASANTLY SWEET INDONESIAN-inspired dish would make a good introduction to shellfish for children. For added color, serve with lime wedges on the side. A shrimp rule of thumb: The larger the size, the longer the cooking time, so if you're working with shrimp smaller than jumbo, adjust your grilling accordingly.

24 jumbo shrimp (about 1½ pounds), peeled and deveined

3 tablespoons molasses

2 tablespoons finely chopped dry-roasted peanuts

Hot steamed white rice

1 tablespoon finely chopped fresh mint

1 tablespoon finely chopped fresh basil

1. Preheat the grill to medium-high and oil the rack. Soak six 12-inch bamboo skewers in water for 30 minutes.

2. Thread the shrimp on skewers (using 4 shrimp per skewer) with space between each shrimp. Grill the shrimp for about 5 minutes each side, or just until just cooked through and opaque, being careful not to overcook. Let the shrimp cool slightly, brush with the molasses, and sprinkle with the peanuts. Arrange the shrimp on plates with the rice and serve sprinkled with the chopped mint and basil.

Serves 6

grilled scallops
with tomato-balsamic salsa

hERE'S THE SCENARIO: YOU'VE RENTED A beach cottage and just picked up the catch of the day from the local seafood shanty. The produce came from a roadside stand that seemed to materialize before your eyes the second you imagined a perfectly ripe tomato. Dinner will be ready in minutes, followed by an evening of stargazing under the clearest night sky you've ever seen.

TOMATO-BALSAMIC SALSA

3 large tomatoes, halved, seeded,
  and cut into small dice
½ red onion, finely chopped
1 tablespoon balsamic vinegar
1 tablespoon olive oil
2 tablespoons finely chopped fresh basil
2 tablespoons finely chopped fresh chives
Salt and freshly ground pepper

2½ to 3 pounds sea scallops, tough side muscle
  removed
Olive oil, for brushing
Salt and freshly ground pepper

1. Make the tomato-balsamic salsa: Combine the tomatoes and onion in a medium bowl. Add the vinegar, oil, basil, and chives; mix well. Season to taste with salt and pepper and set aside. The salsa can be made up to 1 hour ahead and kept, covered, at room temperature.

2. Preheat the grill to medium-high. Soak at least 16 long wooden skewers in warm water for 30 minutes.

3. Double-skewer the scallops to keep them from slipping when you turn them on the grill: Line up 4 or 5 scallops next to each other on a work surface and slip two skewers lengthwise through them, parallel to each other and about ½ inch apart. Repeat with the remaining scallops. Brush the scallops on both sides with olive oil and season with salt and pepper.

4. Brush the grill rack with oil. Place the skewers on the grill and cook for 6 to 8 minutes, turning once, until just opaque throughout.

5. To serve, slide the scallops off the skewers and onto plates; top with the salsa.

Serves 8

chapter five
desserts & drinks

grilled peaches
with red-berry sauce

YOU MAY NOT THINK OF SWEETS WHEN YOU fire up the grill, but hot fire caramelizes the natural sugar in fruit. With the easy berry sauce, these peaches make a superb dessert on their own, but you could turn the dish into a topping for ice cream. In that case, thinly slice each grilled peach half, scatter the slices over vanilla ice cream, and drizzle the sauce over the top.

RED-BERRY SAUCE

½ pint raspberries

Generous 1 cup strawberries, hulled and halved, or quartered if large

2 to 3 tablespoons sugar, preferably superfine, or more to taste

½ to 1 tablespoon Chambord or other berry-flavored liqueur (optional)

4 large ripe peaches, halved and pitted

2 tablespoons unsalted butter, melted

Sugar, for sprinkling

Raspberries, for garnish

8 sprigs of mint, for garnish

1. Make the red-berry sauce: Combine the berries and sugar in a food processor and process to a smooth puree. Strain the puree through a fine strainer to remove the raspberry seeds, pressing on the solids to extract as much sauce as possible. Add more sugar to taste, if needed, and stir in the liqueur. Cover and refrigerate for 1 to 2 hours, or until chilled. The sauce can be made up to 2 days in advance.

2. Preheat the grill to medium-high.

3. Brush the cut sides of the peaches lightly with melted butter and sprinkle lightly with sugar. Place the peaches cut side down on the grill and cook until grill marks appear and the peaches are slightly softened, 3 to 5 minutes.

4. Place 1 peach half on each plate, cut side up, and drizzle the sauce over and around the peaches. Garnish with raspberries and mint sprigs. Serve immediately.

Serves 8

grilled pineapple
with sweet balsamic sauce

DESSERTS
& DRINKS

SINCE THEY DON'T GET ANY SWEETER AFTER picking, pineapples are only harvested when they're ripe, so go ahead and pick up a fresh one at the supermarket. But if you want a sweet sure thing that you can always have on hand in the pantry, try canned pineapple instead. (Remember to decrease the cooking time to just heat the pineapple through.) This is the perfect dessert to make when your grill has cooled down after cooking the entree, because you need to use a low fire.

> ¼ cup firmly packed brown sugar
> 2 tablespoons balsamic vinegar
> Eight ½-inch-thick slices ripe fresh pineapple
> 1 pint vanilla ice cream
> Strawberries on the stem, for garnish

1. Preheat the grill to low and oil the rack.

2. In a small saucepan, cook the sugar and vinegar over low heat, stirring constantly until the sugar dissolves. Increase the heat to high and bring the mixture to a boil. Immediately reduce the heat and simmer for 2 minutes. Keep the sauce warm over low heat until ready to serve.

3. Grill the pineapple slices on the prepared rack set 5 to 6 inches over the coals for 8 minutes. Flip the pineapple slices and cook for 6 minutes, or until the pineapple is golden brown and softened.

4. To serve, arrange 2 pineapple slices on each of four dessert plates, top with a scoop of ice cream, drizzle with the sweet balsamic sauce, and garnish with strawberries.

Fruity Grilling

There is so much you can do with four seasons of fruit on the grill. A few possibilities:

• Grill bananas in their skins, then let guests make their own warm banana splits at an ice cream bar set up near the grill.

• Fill half-cored apples with butter, raisins, and cinnamon; roast over hot coals.

• Lightly brush medium-thick orange and papaya slices with flavorless vegetable oil, then grill.

• Skewer sliced pears and pitted cherries, grill briefly, and serve with gingerbread.

• In a bowl, mix sliced peaches and seedless grapes with sugar and a splash of rum or brandy. Spoon onto squares of foil, fold into packets, then steam on the grill. Open the hot packets carefully.

trade-winds
fruit kebabs

T HE CARIBBEAN MIGHT BECKON, BUT YOUR annual vacation is still months away. For a quick taste of the tropics, fire up the grill and make these festive fruit kebabs. Serve them with a trio of sorbets or arranged on a large platter tiled with pineapple slices.

COCONUT MARINADE

½ cup well-stirred canned coconut milk

2 tablespoons fresh lime juice

2 tablespoons packed light brown sugar

1 teaspoon grated lime zest

3 ripe pineapple slices, ¾ inch thick,
   cut into 6 triangle-shaped wedges each

Twelve 1½-inch-thick slices banana

1 medium papaya, peeled, seeded, and cut into
   ½- by 1-inch pieces

1 medium mango, peeled, halved, seeded, and
   each half cut into 3 long strips

2 small kiwis, peeled, trimmed, and each cut
   into 3 crosswise slices

6 strawberries, hulled

Toasted grated coconut

1. Preheat the grill to medium. Soak six 12-inch wooden skewers in water for 30 minutes.

2. Make the coconut marinade: Stir all the ingredients together in a 9- by 13-inch glass baking dish and let stand for 15 min-

utes. Gently stir in the pineapple, banana, papaya, and mango and marinate at room temperature for 15 minutes, turning occasionally.

3. Thread fruit onto each skewer in the following order: pineapple, papaya, banana, pineapple, mango, banana, papaya, and pineapple.

4. Grill the kebabs for about 10 minutes, turning often. Just before serving thread a kiwi slice and a whole strawberry onto the tip of each skewer. Serve sprinkled with toasted coconut.

Serves 6

strawberry napoleons
amandine

i S THERE A PICK-YOUR-OWN FARM NEARBY? Invite guests for an outing, fill your baskets, then head home to indulge. That strawberries are at their best just a few short weeks of the year makes them all the more special.

> 4 sheets phyllo dough, thawed if frozen
> 4 tablespoons (½ stick) unsalted butter, melted and cooled
> ⅓ cup plus 1 tablespoon sugar
> 2 cups heavy cream
> 1 teaspoon vanilla extract
> 24 ripe small strawberries, hulled and sliced
> ½ cup sliced natural almonds

1. Preheat the oven to 375°F. Butter two baking sheets.

2. Place 1 phyllo sheet on a work surface; brush with 1 tablespoon butter and sprinkle with 4 teaspoons sugar. Repeat the layering with the phyllo, butter, and sugar three more times. Trim the phyllo stack to a 16- by 12-inch rectangle, then cut it into twelve 4-inch squares. Cut each square diagonally in half, making 24 triangles. Transfer the triangles to the prepared baking sheets. Bake for about 10 minutes, or until golden brown. Transfer the triangles to a wire rack to cool.

3. Just before serving, combine the cream, the remaining 1 tablespoon sugar, and the vanilla in a medium bowl; whip just to stiff peaks.

4. Place 1 phyllo triangle in the center of each of 8 plates. Top each triangle with 3 tablespoons of whipped cream and 1 sliced strawberry; add another triangle so the points go in a slightly offset angle from the first and top with berries and cream. Repeat with the remaining triangles, cream, and strawberries. Sprinkle with the almonds.

Serves 8

strawberry buttermilk
shortcake

h ERE'S A DESSERT THAT'S ALL ABOUT CON-
trasts: warm, crisp, and crumbly biscuits set off
by velvety smooth cream and refreshing syrup.
When it's not strawberry season, try the same recipe with
huckleberries or blackberries.

4 pints small ripe strawberries

¼ cup plus 1 teaspoon granulated sugar, or

as needed

2¼ cups unbleached flour

½ cup packed light brown sugar

1½ teaspoons baking powder

1 teaspoon baking soda

¼ teaspoon salt

¼ cup (½ stick) cold unsalted butter, cut

into pieces

¾ cup buttermilk

Whipped cream, for serving

1. Preheat the oven to 425ºF. Butter a large baking sheet.

2. Reserve 6 of the nicest-looking strawberries, with hulls and
stems, if available, for garnish. Hull and slice the remaining
berries. In a large bowl, crush half of the sliced strawberries
with a potato masher or a fork. Stir in the remaining sliced
strawberries and ¼ cup of the granulated sugar, adding more
sugar if necessary, depending on the sweetness of the berries.
Set aside at room temperature.

3. In a large bowl, whisk the flour, brown sugar, baking powder, baking soda, and salt together. Using your fingers, break
up any lumps of brown sugar. With a pastry blender or two
knives, cut in the butter until the mixture resembles coarse
crumbs. With a fork, stir in the buttermilk just until combined;
do not overblend, or the shortcakes might be tough. Form the
dough into a ball; if it is very sticky, add 1 or 2 tablespoons
more flour.

4. Transfer the dough to a floured surface and pat it into a
¾-inch-thick round, about 8 inches in diameter. With a floured
3-inch round cutter, cut out 6 biscuits; you will need to press
together the scraps of dough. Transfer the biscuits to a baking
sheet and sprinkle them with the remaining 1 teaspoon granulated sugar.

5. Bake the biscuits for 12 to 15 minutes, until golden brown.
Transfer to a wire rack and let cool slightly.

6. To serve, split the shortcakes with a fork and place the
bottom half of a biscuit on each of 6 dessert plates. Spoon over
a generous portion of berries and add the biscuit tops. Spoon
on the remaining sliced berries and drizzle the berry juices over
the dessert. Spoon the whipped cream alongside the biscuits,
garnish with the whole berries, and serve immediately.

Serves 6

chocolate-chunk *blondies*

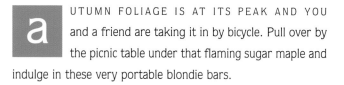

a UTUMN FOLIAGE IS AT ITS PEAK AND YOU and a friend are taking it in by bicycle. Pull over by the picnic table under that flaming sugar maple and indulge in these very portable blondie bars.

I cup (2 sticks) unsalted butter, at room temperature

I ⅔ cups packed dark brown sugar

2 large eggs

I ¼ teaspoons vanilla extract

¼ teaspoon salt

I ¾ cups all-purpose flour

I cup semisweet chocolate chips

1. Preheat the oven to 350°F. Butter a 13- by 9-inch baking pan.

2. In a large bowl, beat the butter and brown sugar with an electric mixer until light and fluffy. Add the eggs one at a time, beating well after each addition. Beat in the vanilla, then beat in the salt. On low speed, beat in the flour in two additions. With a wooden spoon, stir in the chocolate chips. Spread the batter evenly in the prepared pan and smooth the top.

3. Bake for 30 to 35 minutes, until golden brown on top and no longer puffy; do not overbake. Let cool completely in the pan on a wire rack.

4. With a large sharp knife, cut into 24 bars.

Makes 2 dozen bars

berries & custard sauce

t RY THIS SIMPLE HOMEMADE CUSTARD WITH your berry harvest. You can keep the custard, covered and chilled, up to a week—but let it warm slightly before serving, to bring out its flavor. Mix the berries and custard in eggcups or stemmed glasses or pass the custard separately in a small pitcher.

3 large egg yolks

¼ cup sugar

I ¾ cups half-and-half

½ teaspoon vanilla extract

3 to 4 cups ripe blueberries, blackberries, raspberries, and/or sliced strawberries

1. In a medium heatproof bowl, whisk the egg yolks and sugar together. In a medium saucepan, bring the half-and-half just to a simmer. Slowly pour ½ cup of half-and-half into the yolk mixture and whisk until combined well. In a slow, steady stream, pour the remaining half-and-half into the yolks, whisking constantly. Return the mixture to the saucepan and cook, stirring, over low heat just until the mixture coats the back of a wooden spoon. Immediately pour the custard sauce through a strainer into a bowl and stir in the vanilla. Let the sauce cool for at least 5 minutes before serving.

2. Arrange the berries in serving cups and top with the custard. Serve immediately.

Serves 4 to 6

DESSERTS & DRINKS

mocha-bourbon
mud cake

dON'T BE ALARMED: "MUD CAKE" REFERS TO the slightly cracked top of this light-textured dessert, which bears no relation to the dense, rich pies of the same name. On hot summer days when the air itself seems to be melting, you'll appreciate the absence of frosting. We add a dusting of confectioners' sugar (sift through a cake stencil for picture-perfect results) and serve the cake with whipped cream. A scoop of vanilla ice cream would also be good with each slice of cake.

6 ounces unsweetened chocolate, coarsely chopped

3 tablespoons instant espresso powder or instant
coffee granules

1 ¾ cups all-purpose flour

1 ½ teaspoons baking soda

¼ teaspoon salt

1 cup (2 sticks) unsalted butter,
at room temperature

2 cups granulated sugar

4 large eggs, at room temperature

1 ½ teaspoons vanilla extract

½ cup bourbon

Confectioners' sugar and sweetened whipped cream,
for serving

1. Preheat the oven to 350°F. Butter and flour a 10-inch springform pan.

2. Melt the chocolate in the top of a double boiler over gently simmering water or in a microwave; set aside. In a small cup, dissolve the espresso powder in ¼ cup of boiling water.

3. In a medium bowl, whisk together the flour, baking soda, and salt.

4. In a large bowl, beat the butter and sugar until light and fluffy, 2 to 3 minutes. Add the eggs one at a time, beating well after each addition. Beat in the vanilla. On low speed, beat in one third of the flour mixture. Beat in the espresso mixture, then beat in the bourbon. Beat in the remaining flour in 2 additions, alternating with 1 cup water. Pour the batter into the prepared pan and smooth the top.

5. Bake for 55 to 60 minutes, until the top is slightly puffy and a toothpick inserted in the center comes out clean. Let cool completely in the pan on a wire rack.

6. To serve, run a sharp knife around the side of the springform pan. Remove the side of the pan and transfer the cake to a serving platter. The cake will keep, covered, at room temperature for several days. Sprinkle with confectioners' sugar, cut into slices, and serve with whipped cream.

Serves 10

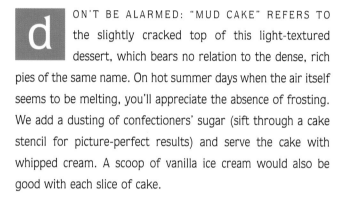

chocolate-mint
icebox cake

tHE BEAUTY OF THIS RETRO-INSPIRED "CAKE" is that it requires no baking, so it's perfect to prepare for a warm weather gathering. When guests see it presented on a pressed-glass pedestal, many will wax nostalgic, remembering how their own aproned mothers would prepare this dessert (sometimes called "zebra pudding") for celebrations in the days when Howdy Doody reigned.

ICEBOX CAKE

2 cups heavy cream

3 tablespoons sugar

½ teaspoon mint extract

One 9-ounce box chocolate wafer cookies

Chocolate shavings, for garnish (see Note)

Chocolate Sauce (page 139)

1. Make the icebox cake: In a large bowl, combine the cream, sugar, and mint extract and beat with an electric mixer until the cream holds stiff peaks.

2. Spread a thin layer (about ¼ inch) of cream over the top of 1 cookie. Spread a second cookie with cream and place on top of the first one. Continue until you have a stack of 8 cookies. Carefully lay the stack on its side across one end of a long platter. Make a second stack of 8 cookies and lay it next to the first one. Continue with the remaining cookies until you have made 5 stacks (you may have a few cookies left over). Using a long metal spatula, generously frost the top and sides of the cookie stacks with the remaining whipped cream. Refrigerate, loosely covered, for at least 6 hours, or overnight, before serving. (The cookies will continue to soften as they stand—how soft you want them is your choice.)

3. Just before serving, sprinkle the cake generously with chocolate shavings. Using a sharp knife, cut the cake on a slight diagonal into thick slices. Lay a slice on each plate and drizzle it with some of the sauce (or pass the sauce separately).

Serves 8 to 10

■ Note

Use a vegetable peeler or the large holes of a box grater to make chocolate shavings from a 1-ounce square of semisweet or bittersweet chocolate.

desserts take a holiday
fourth-of-july tart cart

roll out an Independence Day welcome wagon filled with tempting treats after a backyard meal, and you might even upstage the fireworks display. All you have to do is think red, white, and blue . . . berries! Search your cupboards, the linen closet—even the toy chest—for those three essential colors, and let yourself get carried away with the theme.

TART-CART SELECTIONS

luscious lemon-curd tart
(page 130)

fresh summer blueberry tart
(page 131)

berries & cream crostata
(page 133)

sweet ricotta & plum pizza
(page 134)

SCREAMING FOR ICE CREAM

peach wedges and crumbled amaretto cookies

maple syrup and gingersnaps

sliced bananas and a sprinkle of instant coffee granules

fresh fruit preserves

quartered strawberries and a drizzle of best-quality balsamic vinegar

WHEELED FROM THE GRILL

grilled peaches with red-berry sauce
(page 116)

grilled pineapples with sweet balsamic sauce
(page 118)

trade-winds fruit kebabs
(page 119)

Patriotic Settings

This July 4th, set your table with the works:

- Coat unglazed clay pots with acrylic paint in the day's colors, let dry, then paint details like folk-art stars, squiggly stripes, and polka dots. Use pots to hold flatware, sparklers, or rock-candy swizzle sticks.

- Pair red-handled Bakelite serving ware with Blue Willow china.

- Add small American parade flags to center-pieces. Include stars-and-stripes pinwheels, too. To make brand-new flags look vintage, give them a dip in a weak tea bath.

- Tie ribbon streamers to chair backs; add hand-cut white-paper stars inscribed with each guest's name.

ginger-nectarine
upside-down cake

pUT QUITE SIMPLY, YOUR GUESTS WILL GO crazy for this fruit-topped ginger cake and demand you turn over the recipe. Tell them it came from your Great-Aunt Pearl—the one who ran the penny candy shop up in Maine—and you swore you'd never share it with a soul. Everyone needs to have one closely guarded family recipe, don't you think? Use peaches instead of nectarines if they are at their peak.

GINGER-NECTARINE TOPPING

¼ cup (½ stick) unsalted butter,
    cut into 4 pieces

½ cup packed light brown sugar

3 small to medium nectarines, peeled, pitted,
    and cut into 10 wedges each (see Note)

2 tablespoons minced candied ginger

GINGER CAKE

1⅓ cups all-purpose flour

1½ teaspoons baking powder

½ teaspoon ground ginger

¼ teaspoon salt

½ cup (1 stick) unsalted butter,
    at room temperature

1 cup granulated sugar

2 large eggs, at room temperature

1 teaspoon vanilla extract

½ cup milk

1. Preheat the oven to 350°F.

2. Make the ginger-nectarine topping: In a 9-inch round cake pan, melt the butter over low heat. Add the brown sugar and cook, stirring with a wooden spoon, until the mixture is gently bubbling and smooth, 3 to 4 minutes (it may look slightly grainy). Remove from heat. Arrange the nectarine slices side by side in a ring on top of the brown sugar mixture, about ½ inch from the sides of the pan. Arrange several slices in a design in the center, cutting them to fit if necessary. (If you have a few nectarine slices left over, toss them in lemon juice—to prevent discoloration—and add to salads or fruit compotes.) Sprinkle the ginger over and around the nectarines. Set aside.

3. Make the ginger cake: In a medium bowl, whisk together the flour, baking powder, ginger, and salt.

4. In a large bowl, beat the butter and sugar with an electric mixer until light and fluffy, 2 to 3 minutes. Add the eggs one at a time, beating well after each addition. Beat in the vanilla. On low speed, beat in half the flour mixture. Beat in the milk, then beat in the remaining flour mixture.

5. Spoon the batter over the nectarines and, using a rubber spatula, carefully spread it evenly over the fruit, making sure the batter touches the sides of the pan all around. Bake for 45 to 50 minutes, until a toothpick inserted into the center of the cake comes out clean.

6. Let the cake cool in the pan on a rack for 3 minutes. Run a knife around the sides of the pan to release the cake from the

pan, invert a rimmed serving plate over the top of the pan, and invert the cake and pan onto the plate. Lift off the pan. If any nectarine slices have stuck to the bottom of the pan, replace them on top of the cake. Let cool slightly. Serve the cake warm or at room temperature.

Serves 8

■ Note

To peel nectarines or peaches, immerse them in boiling water for 30 seconds to 1 minute, then peel off the skin with your fingers and/or a paring knife.

luscious
lemon-curd tart

ONCE AGAIN, WE'VE TAKEN A SNEAKY SHORT-cut with this recipe, using jarred lemon curd (right next to jams and jellies at the market) instead of making it from scratch. But you'll appreciate the convenience when you're in a crunch, with guests pulling in the driveway for a long weekend just as you're unloading the groceries from the trunk. If you're really in a time bind, you could even use a prepared crust—we won't tell a soul.

DESSERTS
& DRINKS

SWEET TART SHELL

1¼ cups all-purpose flour

¼ cup confectioners' sugar

Generous pinch of salt

6 tablespoons (¾ stick) cold unsalted butter, cut into ½-inch cubes

LEMON-CURD FILLING

1½ cups heavy cream

3 tablespoons granulated sugar

One 10- to 11-ounce jar good-quality lemon curd

Raspberries, for garnish

1. Make the sweet tart shell: In a food processor, combine the flour, confectioners' sugar, and salt and pulse until blended. Scatter the butter over the flour and pulse 10 to 15 times, until the mixture resembles coarse meal. Add 2½ tablespoons ice water and pulse until the dough just starts to come together, adding up to 1 tablespoon more water if necessary;

do not overmix the dough. Shape the dough into a disk, wrap in plastic, and refrigerate for at least 30 minutes or overnight.

2. On a lightly floured surface, roll out the dough to a 12½-inch round. Fit the dough into a 10-inch fluted tart pan with a removable bottom and trim the excess dough even with the top edge of the pan. Refrigerate the shell for 30 minutes.

3. Preheat the oven to 375°F.

4. Blind bake the tart shell: Line the tart shell with foil and fill with dried beans or raw rice. Bake for 15 minutes. Remove the foil and weights and bake for 8 to 10 minutes longer, until the pastry is golden brown. Transfer to a wire rack and let cool completely. The tart shell can be made up to 1 day ahead and stored, covered, at room temperature.

5. Make the lemon-curd filling: In a large bowl, combine the cream and sugar and beat with an electric mixer until the cream just barely starts to hold firm peaks. Using a large rubber spatula, gradually fold in the lemon curd until just combined. Transfer the filling to the cooled tart shell and smooth the top. Refrigerate for at least 2 hours before serving. The tart can be made up to 6 hours in advance.

6. To serve, remove the sides of the tart pan, cut the tart into wedges, and garnish with raspberries.

Serves 8

fresh summer
blueberry tart

S UMMER HIKERS KNOW THAT WOODLAND blueberries are so far superior to cultivated that it's worth going on a trek just to find them. Time your expedition for July through August, when blueberries ripen. Bring a few pails and a couple of kids—they love picking berries and are just the right size for gathering low-bush types. Remember to freeze some, and you'll be able to keep summer going all winter long. Serve this tart with vanilla ice cream if you want to gild the lily.

BLUEBERRY FILLING

1 quart blueberries

1 teaspoon freshly grated lemon zest

2 tablespoons cornstarch

Scant 1 cup sugar

⅛ teaspoon salt

One baked 10-inch tart shell, made with Sweet Tart Shell (page 130)

1. Make the blueberry filling: In a food processor, process 1 cup of the blueberries until finely chopped, scraping down the sides of the bowl once or twice. Transfer the chopped berries to a large saucepan. Put the remaining berries in a large bowl and add the lemon zest; set aside.

2. Combine the cornstarch and 2 tablespoons of water in a small cup, stirring until smooth. Add 6 tablespoons water, the sugar, and salt to the saucepan of chopped blueberries and

bring to a boil over medium heat, stirring occasionally. Stir the cornstarch mixture, add it to the pan, and bring back to a boil, stirring constantly. Boil, stirring, for 1 minute.

3. Pour the hot blueberry mixture over the whole berries, stirring gently with a rubber spatula until all the berries are evenly coated. Pour the mixture into the prepared tart shell and smooth the top. Refrigerate for at least 2 hours, or until the filling is cooled and set. The tart can be covered loosely and refrigerated for up to 8 hours.

4. To serve, remove the sides of the tart pan and cut the tart into wedges.

Serves 8 to 10

berries & cream
crostata

FILLED WITH LUSH PASTRY CREAM AND RIPE berries, this tart is perfect all spring and summer. Bake the shell in the morning, before the day's heat sets in, and finish the tart just before serving.

TART SHELL

1½ cups all-purpose flour

3 tablespoons granulated sugar

¼ teaspoon salt

½ cup (1 stick) chilled unsalted butter,
    cut into small pieces

PASTRY CREAM

1 cup milk

⅓ cup granulated sugar

3 large egg yolks, lightly beaten

2 tablespoons cornstarch

2 tablespoons butter

1 teaspoon vanilla extract

BERRY TOPPING

½ cup heavy cream

3 cups ripe blueberries and/or blackberries

3 cups sliced ripe strawberries

Confectioners' sugar, for dusting

1. Preheat the oven to 425°. Make the tart shell: In a bowl, stir the flour, sugar, and salt together until well combined. Cut in the butter until pieces are the size of small peas. Stirring con-

stantly with a fork, add 4 to 5 tablespoons ice water very slowly until the dough just begins to come together, stopping before it becomes a solid mass. Press the dough together and knead slightly; form into a 7-inch disk.

2. On a floured surface, roll out the dough to a 14-inch round. With a floured rolling pin, transfer to an 11-inch tart pan with a removable bottom. Fold the overhang in and press it against side so the edge is a double thickness. Blind bake (see step 4, page 130) with weights for 15 to 20 minutes. Remove weights; bake for 10 minutes more. Cool on a wire rack.

3. Make the pastry cream: In a small saucepan, combine ¾ cup of the milk and the sugar. Bring to a boil over medium heat, stirring to dissolve the sugar. Pour the remaining ¼ cup milk into a bowl, add the egg yolks and cornstarch, and whisk until smooth. Whisk the boiling milk mixture into the yolk mixture. Return to the pan and cook, whisking constantly, until the mixture comes to a boil, taking care that the whisk reaches all corners of the pan. Boil for 1 minute. Remove from the heat; whisk in the butter and vanilla. Let cool to room temperature. Transfer to a small bowl and chill, covered, until cold.

4. Just before serving, in a large bowl, whip the cream just to stiff peaks. Whisk the pastry cream until smooth; fold in the whipped cream. In another bowl, gently toss the berries. Fill the tart shell with the pastry cream and top with berries; sprinkle with confectioners' sugar. Serve immediately.

Serves 8 to 10

sweet ricotta &
plum pizza

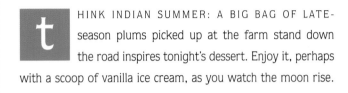

THINK INDIAN SUMMER: A BIG BAG OF LATE-season plums picked up at the farm stand down the road inspires tonight's dessert. Enjoy it, perhaps with a scoop of vanilla ice cream, as you watch the moon rise.

SWEET PIZZA DOUGH

1⅓ cups all-purpose flour

½ cup sugar

1 tablespoon baking powder

Pinch of salt

⅔ cup ricotta cheese

2 tablespoons chilled unsalted butter,
   cut into small pieces

1 large egg yolk

2 teaspoons milk

1¼ teaspoons vanilla extract

1 large egg white, lightly beaten

6 to 8 (about 1½ pounds) ripe purple and/or
   red plums, halved, pitted, and each half cut
   into ½-inch-thick wedges

3 tablespoons granulated sugar

1. Make the sweet pizza dough: In a food processor, combine the flour, sugar, baking powder, and salt and pulse to blend.

2. Add the ricotta, butter, egg yolk, milk, and vanilla and pulse just until the dough begins to come together. Shape the dough into a disk.

3. Chill the dough, wrapped in waxed paper, for at least 1 hour or up to 3 days.

4. Preheat the oven to 350°F. Butter a large baking sheet.

5. Between two sheets of waxed paper, roll out the pizza dough with a rolling pin to a 10-inch circle. Remove the top sheet of waxed paper, transfer the dough to the prepared pan, paper side up, and remove the remaining sheet of paper. Fold in the edge to make a ½-inch rim.

6. Bake the pizza crust for 10 minutes. Remove from the oven and brush the top of the crust with the egg white. Fan the plum slices on the dough, starting at the edge and ringing the perimeter, arranging them with the skin side down. Working toward the center, fan the slices in smaller and smaller circles until all of the dough is covered. Sprinkle the sugar evenly over the plums and bake for 1 hour, or until the crust is golden brown and the plums are cooked through. Remove from the oven and let stand for at least 5 minutes.

7. To serve, cut the warm pizza into wedges and serve.

Serves 10 to 12

double-coconut
lemon pie

a FTER YOU'VE SERVED OUR PIQUANT MANGO & Chicken Salad (page 87) to your guests, follow up with this delectable concoction that requires minimal baking skills. The shell couldn't be easier—it's just toasted coconut, pure and simple. The refreshing filling is a sort of tropical freeze; if you'd like, you could substitute lime or orange sorbet (or a combination of the two) for the lemon. If children will share the dessert, leave out the rum.

COCONUT SHELL

One 7-ounce package sweetened flaked coconut

LEMON FILLING

2 pints lemon sorbet, softened

6 tablespoons cream of coconut (shake the can well before opening and measuring)

1 tablespoon dark or light rum

1. Preheat the oven to 325°F.

2. Make the shell: Put the coconut in a large bowl and break up any clumps with your fingertips. Press the coconut evenly over the bottom and up the side of a 9-inch glass pie plate. Bake for 12 to 15 minutes, until the edges of the crust are golden brown. Cool completely on a wire rack.

3. Make the lemon filling: In a large bowl, combine the sorbet, coconut cream, and rum and blend well with a wooden spoon. Cover and freeze just until firm enough to spread, 15 to 30 minutes.

4. Spread the sorbet mixture evenly in the cooled crust. Freeze until firm, at least 4 hours, or overnight, before serving.

Serves 8

DESSERTS
& DRINKS

three-sorbet
terrine

WE ALL KNOW SOMEONE WHO MAKES HER OWN sorbet (not to mention her own breakfast muffins and croutons). But that doesn't mean we have to. In reality, you can get wonderful results from supermarket sorbets. Just choose contrasting flavors and colors such as mango, lemon, and raspberry, and nestle them together in a terrine arrangement. Garnish with a drizzle of chocolate sauce or fresh strawberries and kiwi slices. Sorbets are the ultimate palate cleansers when they're made with acidic ingredients.

3 sorbets of complementary colors and flavors (about 1⅓ cups of each)

1. Let the sorbets stand at room temperature just long enough to soften to a spreadable consistency.

2. In an 8½- by 4½-inch terrine or loaf pan, spread the first sorbet evenly so the pan is about one-third full. Top with an even layer of the second sorbet, then the third sorbet. Cover with plastic wrap and freeze for at least 4 hours or overnight, until very firm.

3. To serve, remove the terrine from the freezer and let it stand for several minutes. Run a table knife around the edge, invert the pan onto a platter, and remove the pan. Cut the terrine crosswise into thick slices.

Serves 8

purple plum
granita

GRANITAS ARE LIKE A SNOW CONE WITH THE intense flavor of a sorbet. Don't scoop this dessert, serve it by raking along the top with a fork to give a fluffiness to the crystals.

6 ripe red purple plums (about 1½ pounds), pitted and sliced
¾ cup sugar
1 tablespoon fresh lemon juice

1. Place a 9-inch square baking pan in the freezer.

2. In the bowl of a food processor, pulse the plums until they are very finely chopped. Transfer the plums to a large bowl.

3. In a small saucepan, bring 2 cups water and the sugar to a boil over high heat, stirring constantly; boil 2 minutes, or until the sugar has dissolved. Pour syrup over plums; let stand 20 minutes. Add lemon juice; let cool. Chill, covered, for 2 hours.

4. Pour mixture through a strainer into the cold baking pan, pressing on solids to extract as much liquid as possible; discard solids. Cover pan with foil and freeze for 1 hour, or until ice forms around the edge. Scrape the ice with a fork to combine with liquid. Repeat every 30 minutes for 2½ hours, or until mixture forms a smooth consistency of identifiable ice crystals.

5. Serve the granita at once, or hold for 4 hours and stir once or twice to break up any clumps.

Serves 4 to 6

ice cream &
cherry sauce

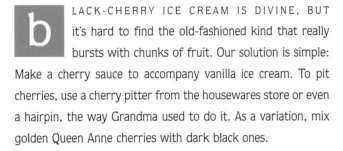

b LACK-CHERRY ICE CREAM IS DIVINE, BUT it's hard to find the old-fashioned kind that really bursts with chunks of fruit. Our solution is simple: Make a cherry sauce to accompany vanilla ice cream. To pit cherries, use a cherry pitter from the housewares store or even a hairpin, the way Grandma used to do it. As a variation, mix golden Queen Anne cherries with dark black ones.

CHERRY SAUCE

3 tablespoons unsalted butter

1½ pounds ripe cherries, pitted

6 tablespoons sugar

2 pints good-quality vanilla ice cream

1. Make the cherry sauce: Melt the butter in a large deep skillet over medium heat. Add the cherries and cook, stirring frequently, until they start to release their juices, 3 to 5 minutes. Sprinkle the sugar over the cherries and cook, stirring, until the sugar has dissolved and the juices have thickened slightly, 3 to 5 minutes longer. Remove from the heat and let cool slightly, or cool to room temperature. The sauce can be made up to 2 days ahead and kept, covered, in the refrigerator. Before serving, reheat over low heat, stirring occasionally.

2. To serve, scoop the ice cream into bowls or goblets and spoon the sauce over the top.

Serves 8

cantaloupe
ice cream

g ORGEOUS AS IS, THIS CAN BE EVEN BETTER looking served garnished with cookies and tiny melon balls of assorted colors, and sliced strawberries, fresh ripe blackberries, or raspberries.

½ cup sugar

2 tablespoons anisette or other anise liqueur

Two 3-inch strips lemon zest

1 tablespoon fresh lemon juice

1 ripe cantaloupe, peeled, seeded, and chopped

½ cup heavy cream

1. In a medium saucepan, bring ½ cup water, the sugar, the anisette, and the zest to a boil, stirring until the sugar has dissolved. Reduce the heat and simmer the mixture for 5 minutes. Stir in the lemon juice, transfer the syrup to a bowl, and let cool to room temperature. Chill, covered, for about 1 hour, or until very cold.

2. In a blender or the bowl of a food processor, puree the cantaloupe, scraping down the sides with a rubber spatula. Add the syrup and the heavy cream and pour the mixture through a strainer, pressing hard on the solids to extract as much of the liquid as possible. Chill the mixture, covered, for about 2 hours, or until it is very cold.

3. Freeze in an ice cream maker according to the manufacturers' instructions.

Serves 4 to 6

banana "ice cream"
with chocolate sauce

tALK ABOUT INSTANT GRATIFICATION. THIS dessert is ready in minutes. If you keep a jar of chocolate sauce on hand and some bananas in the freezer, you'll never be without a homemade treat to bring out for unexpected guests or just to indulge yourself as you laze in the hammock on a Saturday afternoon.

BANANA "ICE CREAM"

8 large ripe bananas

⅔ cup sour cream

⅓ cup sugar, preferably superfine

Generous ½ teaspoon vanilla extract

CHOCOLATE SAUCE

3 ounces bittersweet or semisweet chocolate,
  coarsely chopped

⅔ cup heavy cream

¼ cup sugar

1. Peel the bananas and cut into large chunks. Put in an airtight container and freeze for 3 to 4 hours, until firm. (The bananas can be frozen overnight, but they will start to discolor if frozen for much longer.)

2. Meanwhile, make the chocolate sauce: Combine the chocolate, cream, and sugar in a small heavy saucepan and heat over low heat, stirring, until the chocolate has melted and the sauce is smooth. Remove from the heat and let cool slightly, or refrigerate and serve cold. The sauce can be made up to 3 days ahead and kept, covered, in the refrigerator; let it come to room temperature or rewarm briefly over low heat, if desired.

3. Make the banana "ice cream": If the bananas are very hard, let them sit at room temperature for about 10 minutes to soften slightly. In two batches, combine the bananas, sour cream, sugar, and vanilla in a food processor and process until smooth (it's fine if there are a few bits of banana still visible). The ice cream can be served immediately (it will be fairly soft) or transferred to an airtight container and frozen for up to 3 hours.

4. To serve, scoop the ice cream into small bowls and drizzle the sauce over the top.

Serves 8

strawberries
romanoff lemonade

DESSERTS
& DRINKS

tHIS IS NOT THE DRINK YOU SOLD AT YOUR first lemonade stand. But it would be kinda fun to set up a lemonade stand on your patio where guests can serve themselves and garnish to their hearts' content: Offer orange zest strips and strawberries threaded onto skewers. Or freeze whole raspberries, knotted strips and twists of citrus peel, and mint leaves inside ice cubes. Here's to summer pleasures: Clink!

½ cup fresh lemon juice (from about 3 lemons)

½ lemon, thinly sliced

6 tablespoons sugar

1 pint strawberries, hulled and sliced

½ cup orange juice, preferably fresh

1. In a pitcher, combine 1½ cups of water, the lemon juice, the lemon slices, and the sugar, stirring until the sugar has dissolved.

2. In a blender, puree half of the strawberries with the orange juice. Pour the mixture through a fine strainer into the pitcher. Stir in the remaining strawberries. Serve in tall glasses over plenty of ice.

Serves 4

Retro-Bar Fun

Let's face it: The hostess with the mostess is the one who can always hand out the right drink in the right glass, no matter how outlandish the request. Equip your outdoor bar with the works—including vintage barware collectibles—for a spot of retro refreshment.

- Use a stoneware crock as an ice bucket. To absorb the drips as the stoneware sweats, wrap a vintage dishtowel around it. Place a folded terrycloth towel beneath the crock.

- Don't avoid plastic, especially if serving drinks poolside. Fifties and sixties nonbreakables can still be found in secondhand shops.

- Look for sets of cocktail glasses from the fifties that came in wirework caddies. They would look great on a bar lit by a space-age standing lamp from the same era.

- Bring out the chrome 1940s Osterizer. Many vintage blenders still work like a charm, and they're a nice match for retro cocktail shakers.

DESSERTS
& DRINKS

sangria
blanca

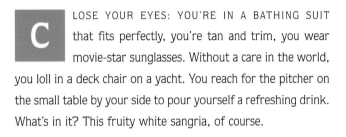

CLOSE YOUR EYES: YOU'RE IN A BATHING SUIT that fits perfectly, you're tan and trim, you wear movie-star sunglasses. Without a care in the world, you loll in a deck chair on a yacht. You reach for the pitcher on the small table by your side to pour yourself a refreshing drink. What's in it? This fruity white sangria, of course.

2 bottles dry white wine

½ cup peach brandy

6 tablespoons sugar, preferably superfine

2 cups club soda

2 ripe peaches, pitted and cut into thin wedges

2 oranges, halved lengthwise, cut crosswise into thin slices, and seeded

I large lemon, cut into thin slices and seeded

Fresh mint sprigs, for garnish

1. In a large pitcher or large deep bowl, combine the wine, brandy, and sugar, stirring to dissolve the sugar. Add the club soda, then add the fruit and stir well. Cover and refrigerate for 2 hours, or until thoroughly chilled.

2. Place 2 or 3 ice cubes in each of eight large wineglasses. Ladle the sangria and fruit into the glasses, garnish with mint sprigs, and serve. Keep the remaining sangria chilled, for refills.

Serves 8

fun faux
sangria

GET OPTIMAL FLAVOR FROM THIS MELANGE by letting the sliced fruit steep in the peach juice for a couple of hours at room temperature. Just for fun, serve it in fifties hobnail drinking glasses, old-fashioned Swanky Swig tumblers decorated with dogs and roosters, or collectible cartoon-character glasses.

6 cups peach juice or nectar

2 firm but ripe peaches, peeled, pitted, and thinly sliced

Two ½-pint containers ripe raspberries

I small orange, trimmed, halved through the stem, cut into thin slices, and seeded

I lemon, trimmed, halved through the stem, cut into thin slices, and seeded

4 cups plain seltzer or club soda

1. In 1 or 2 large pitchers, stir together the peach juice, sliced peaches, raspberries, and orange and lemon slices. The sangria can be prepared several hours ahead to this point and stored, covered, in the refrigerator.

2. To serve, add the seltzer and serve in glasses over ice, with spoons, if desired.

Serves 8 to 10

margarita
coolers

aLTHOUGH NOT AS POTENT AS TRADITIONAL margaritas, these tall refreshing drinks do still have a kick. The fresh lemon-lime base is delicious, but you could substitute two quarts of prepared lemonade, limeade, or lemon-limeade.

1½ cups fresh lemon juice **(6 to 8 lemons)**
½ cup fresh lime juice **(4 to 5 limes)**
1 cup sugar, preferably superfine, or to taste
    (see Note)
1 cup tequila
¾ cup Triple Sec or orange-flavored liqueur
Lime wedges, for garnish

1. In a large pitcher, combine 6 cups of cold water, the lemon juice, lime juice, and sugar, stirring to dissolve the sugar. Refrigerate for 1 hour, or until chilled.

2. Add the tequila and Triple Sec and stir well. Pour into tall ice-filled glasses, garnish each with a lime wedge, and serve immediately.

Serves 8

■ Note

If you don't have superfine sugar, simply grind granulated sugar until fine in a food processor.

sparkling
bellinis

tHE BELLINI, A LOVELY, REFRESHING PEACH-scented drink, was invented at the world-famous Harry's Bar in Venice, Italy. There it is made with a puree of white peaches, so do use that if you are lucky enough to come across it.

3 medium-to-large ripe peaches
Superfine sugar, to taste
One 750-ml bottle Prosecco or other dry
    sparkling white wine

1. To peel the peaches, bring a large pot of water to a boil. Add the peaches and blanch for 30 seconds, then immediately transfer to a cutting board (if the peaches are not ripe, you may need to return them to the boiling water briefly to loosen the skins). Using your fingers and/or a sharp paring knife, peel the peaches, then halve, pit, and coarsely chop them.

2. Transfer the peaches to a food processor and process to a smooth puree. Add sugar to taste, if desired, and process to blend. Transfer 1½ cups of the puree to a large pitcher, cover, and refrigerate until thoroughly chilled (reserve any extra puree for another use, if desired).

3. To serve, gradually add the Prosecco to the peach puree, gently stirring until well blended. Pour into chilled champagne flutes or small glasses and serve immediately.

Serves 8

index